MW01291070

FINDING *My* SECOND WIND

Shannon -
Welcome to this new
life season where discoveries
come and faith deepens as you
continue running the race God has
set before you. Keep your eyes
fixed on Him and trust the
journey. He has the Best
plan for your life.
Finish Strong!

FINDING *My* SECOND WIND

*Running Through Difficult Pain
Finishing Strong with Warrior Faith*

ERIN LEOPOLD

8-29-23

XULON ELITE

Xulon Press Elite
2301 Lucien Way #415
Maitland, FL 32751
407.339.4217
www.xulonpress.com

© 2023 by Erin Leopold

All rights reserved solely by the author. The author guarantees all contents are original and do not infringe upon the legal rights of any other person or work. No part of this book may be reproduced in any form without the permission of the author. The views expressed in this book are not necessarily those of the publisher.

Due to the changing nature of the Internet, if there are any web addresses, links, or URLs included in this manuscript, these may have been altered and may no longer be accessible. The views and opinions shared in this book belong solely to the author and do not necessarily reflect those of the publisher. The publisher, therefore, disclaims responsibility for the views or opinions expressed within the work.

Unless otherwise indicated, Scripture quotations taken from the Holy Bible, New International Version (NIV). Copyright © 1973, 1978, 1984, 2011 by Biblica, Inc.™. Used by permission. All rights reserved.

Paperback ISBN-13: 978-1-66287-268-6

Ebook ISBN-13: 978-1-66287-269-3

Dedication

◇◇◇◇◇◇◇◇◇◇◇◇◇◇◇◇◇◇◇

First and foremost, this is God's story, and I am humbled by the opportunity to partner with Him because of His grace and mercy extended to me and any who choose to receive Jesus Christ as their personal Lord and Savior.

Second, I'd like to thank and dedicate this book to my family without whose love, support, compassion, encouragement, and sacrifice, none of this would be possible. To you, Mom and Dad: your unconditional love and servants' hearts have poured into my life, and I'm forever thankful. To my husband who has stood by me through every season of life, you are my constant love, companion, and friend. Thank you for honoring my story, even when it's hard to understand.

To my three children– my "ABC's"–you have been the heartbeat of my life. On the roughest days when I wanted to quit, you kept me going. Being your mom has been one of the richest blessings of my life. Keep shining bright and remember one bad day with Jesus is better than a lifetime of good days without Him.

And to all those suffering with any form of invisible illness, always know that you are not alone. There is always hope! Keep taking that next step. Run YOUR race and Finish Strong.

Introduction

◇◇◇◇◇◇◇◇◇◇◇◇◇◇◇◇◇◇◇◇

Finding My Second Wind is my personal journey of healing the spirit, soul, and body from a long struggle with chronic disease. My story shares the transforming power you too can have in your life if you're willing to go the extra mile by partnering with God.

I will take you along my bumpy road of faith and endurance as a young athlete who had everything going for her until one day she didn't. Living with any sort of invisible illness, whether it's in our physical bodies, minds, or spirits can be an incredibly dark and lonely road. We often feel misunderstood and wrestle between living based on how we tell ourselves to feel versus how we actually feel. Living in truth requires deepening roots of trust with the Lord to help us heal into wholeness. Going against the grain of a victim mentality by walking the narrow road is a bold choice. I believe too many people quit right before the miracle or breakthrough comes. My hope is that my story will inspire and encourage you to NEVER EVER GIVE UP and will equip you to be the most excellent version of the person God destined you to be.

Table of Contents

Chapter 1

But You Don't Look Sick

Tension fills the air and butterflies engulf my stomach as I sit, yet again, in another doctor's office, anxiously awaiting answers. How many hours have I spent in the waiting room of a medical facility over the past two years? I've lost count. During that time, I've undergone a lengthy series of bloodwork, paperwork questionnaires, MRIs, ultrasounds, and various other forms of poking and prodding. And yet, I have no diagnosis I can depend on.

This visit feels different, though, like a weight so big that if it were a rock falling on me, it would crush me to pieces. My heart is beating so fast that it feels like it is going to explode right out of my chest. My mind continues to ruminate on what this doctor might say and if I will be able to handle another disappointment. This visit is my final stop on the endless tour of searching for answers. I'm not sure where else to go if this doctor can't give me what I need. This is Duke Medical University in 1989, the place reserved for "really sick" people who are desperate to find solutions that local doctors are not able to discover. Duke is known worldwide for its expert medical staff and their ability to help patients who are often without answers and feeling at the end of their rope. This is where I find myself after exhausting local doctors in my area.

I am so thankful my mother can travel with me today, not only to drive but also to give moral support. Being 19 years old and not knowing much about insurance companies and all that goes along with being a grown up, I am relieved to know that I have help. My mom is my rock and accompanies me to most of my appointments. I don't know what I would do without her or the rest of my family who gives me so much support. I know she and my dad are doing the best that they can because it hurts them seeing me like this too. I'm burdened for them as well. We all feel like fish out of water. I hate this for everyone! I can tell how especially hard it's been on Mom, though, as she and I pray for some solid answers and solutions today to my ongoing health crisis. We both will be satisfied just to have a recognizable name that warrants clear cut answers. Knowledge is power and allows for forward motion. Some days, I think I want it more for her than I do for myself because I can tell she feels helpless. Every mom, I believe, feels her child's pain like it is her own. No one can help ease pain like a mother, and mine is that soft place to fall whether I need an encouraging word or a warm hug at the end of a stressful day.

My current diagnosis doesn't seem to carry much value in the world of Western medicine. Chronic mono and Epstein-Barr virus are the main diagnoses given by my family physician after I unexpectedly became very sick about two years ago during my junior year of high school. I had recently moved to South Carolina from Ohio, and it was my family's 10th move. I came down with mononucleosis, which many young people contract, but mine lasted an abnormally long amount of time—five months to be exact. I went from being an active high-ranking student and athlete to one who could barely get out of bed. I had spent the past couple of years going to doctors approved by my insurance company only to find constant dead ends.

"There's really not much we can do for her," the doctors would tell my mom. "Give it time and make sure she gets plenty of rest and drinks lots of water."

Those were things I was already doing, and, in my opinion, unacceptable and dumb answers. No doctor gave me any concrete solutions to my problem, and since I am a "fixer" by nature, this drove me to seek out help outside of my hometown. I began researching places that were within driving distance as I wasn't willing to accept a scenario of doom and gloom, and I was finally able to persuade my family physician to refer me to Duke for a second opinion.

Mom and I patiently sit in the beautifully furnished waiting room of Duke Medical Center. There are dozens of seating arrangements with comfortable fabric-covered royal blue chairs throughout, and since we like looking at the door, we seat ourselves in the back corner where we have a clear view forward. The glass-outlined coffee and end tables display many of my favorite magazines including *Seventeen,* but I feel too sick even to flip though the advertisements. As I look through all my paperwork one more time making sure everything is filled out properly and nothing is missed, I wonder how many more times I will have to go down this path. I hope and pray today is the last day! People crowd in the waiting area, and I wonder which ones are the patients and why they are here. Did they drive four hours one way like I did, or did they travel across the country by plane?

"I wish I would break out in awful spots or some sort of rash, something, anything that could at least get me some sympathy and a doctor to believe me," I said to my mom.

"Oh honey, I am so sorry," she replied. "I can't imagine what that must feel like, but I understand what you mean. Your dad and I believe you because we have seen you go from this energetic, active, vibrant young lady to someone who can't do much of anything. You don't look like anything is wrong with you because you do such a great job of hiding it. You've never been one to complain, so I'm afraid that it's hard for people to really believe you sometimes."

"I know," I responded with tears filling my eyes. "I don't know how else to be except for myself."

"Be you," Mom said as she leaned in and wrapped her arms around me tightly. "God is going to get you through this so keep trusting Him. He has a great plan for your life, and we may not understand now how this fits into it. He promises to work all things together for good for those who love Him and are called according to His purpose."

"Thank you, Mom," I answered. "I know He does but right now I don't feel very loved even though I know I am."

We never know what another person is truly going through simply by judging what we can see with our naked eyes. I learned quickly from my experience that "invisible illness" is real. Even though I look fine on the outside and many people comment, "but you look good," I am suffering greatly on the inside. We should always extend kindness and grace. And just because someone is young like me doesn't mean that they are naturally healthy. Love reaches deep into the unseen places and says *I see you and I hear you.*

As Mom and I continue to sit quietly, I grow more stressed, anxious, and afraid. I hate this. I want to be out enjoying life like other people my age. This isn't fair. I want to be on my favorite six mile run loop listening to "Pump Up the Jam" or back playing midfield on my college club soccer team. The butterflies are churning again, and I feel nauseous enough to vomit. I may need a bathroom soon if someone doesn't hurry up and call me back.

It's only been 30 minutes, but every minute seems to be an hour. What is taking so long? Don't these people know that my time is valuable and that I don't feel well?

I want to run several days a week like I'm used to and play competitive soccer again. My muscles are so weak that walking from the mailbox to the house is too much for me and requires a time-out to lie down. I feel like I run five miles every time I try to do simple activities. Taking a shower is too much from start to finish, so I take many sit-down breaks in between the phases of shampooing, body washing, and conditioning. My breathing labors like a sedentary person who never exercises. You know, the one who smokes several packs of cigarettes a day and huffs and puffs walking up a small hill? My throat is sore and scratchy, and headaches persist daily with no end in sight.

I need to be able to think clearly so that I can make it through college. My brain feels fuzzy, and I struggle to find words that used to come easily to me. I feel dazed and confused, similar to how I would imagine an elderly dementia sufferer must feel. I forget simple things like following directions to places as familiar as home. The achiness in my body never seems to go away, making it difficult to concentrate on much of anything except the chronic pain that inhabits my joints. At times, the hairs on my head hurt if that's even possible. It's taking every ounce of energy I have to sit here and be patient when all I want is to crawl into my bed. I think I'm about to cry, so the best way I know to calm myself down is to pray. I close my eyes and talk to God. I need answers, and I am determined to get them. I am expecting God to show up in BIG ways.

*God, I don't think I can do this anymore. I want my
life back. I'm really scared that no one is going to be
able to help me fix this, and I'll be stuck like this forever. So far, no doctors at home have really been able
to help me get better. I'm scared and mad. I hate this!
Please help me find answers today because I feel like
no one believes me, and they're talking behind my
back saying, "What's wrong with her?" Please bring
me the right doctor and one who not only is a great
physician but also a Christian. I don't understand
why any of this is happening to me, and it's awful. I
promise I'll walk closer to You if I can just feel better
so that it's easier for me to do. Having my health
taken away from me has been the hardest thing ever.
Please give me answers today, God, so that I can get
better. I will do whatever it takes.*

"Erin, come on back."

Mom and I get to our feet and begin making our way to the
door where the nurse introduces herself as Kathy. We make small
talk as we walk down the long narrow corridor to my room, but
it's mostly Mom doing the talking because I'm too nervous and
sick. When I'm not feeling well, I tend to keep it inside and
remain expressionless. I've learned again and again that since I
don't look sick, my words don't seem to carry much persuasion.
So, I keep my mouth shut and merely grin.

"Come in and sit down," says my nurse who points to the
paper covered exam table. "How are you doing today?"

"Terrible," I reply because I am. Why sugar coat my misery? If
I was good, then I wouldn't be here. Mom gives me "the look" to

be nice and act appreciative. I know it's not their fault, but right now I'm mad at the world.

The exam room is nothing special, and to be honest, I was expecting a little more since this place is so well known. There is the standard exam table with two armless chairs and that glaring overhead light that accentuates all your flaws. Why can't someone make these rooms less sterile and more inviting? It's nerve-racking enough to be here without also feeling like an uninvited house guest.

Kathy is flipping through pages of symptoms and notes that I filled out before coming. She and I exchange comments as she goes down the list, trying to make sense of it all before taking my vitals. My blood pressure is still elevated at 138/84 which is way above my normal 105/60. It's been going high like this for a while now because my body is fighting through constant infection, the doctors told me. My oxygen is good, my weight is perfect, and my pulse is running about 15 beats higher because of the nerves.

"OK," she says, "I think I have everything here I need, so sit tight and the doctor will be with you shortly. Today, you will be seeing Dr. Smith. You'll really like him."

"Thank you," I reply with a forced smile.

A few minutes pass, and Dr. Smith enters the room, greeting us both individually. He's an ordinary-looking guy, but the way he talks makes me assume he's smart.

"I've looked over all your recent notes and bloodwork, and I believe you have what's called chronic fatigue syndrome or CFS for short. We don't know much about this illness except that it seems to target highly-stressed and active people like yourself. It can result from a previous virus, and I see that you had a bad case of mononucleosis along with Epstein-Barr two years ago. We don't really know what perpetuates the chronic fatigue, but patients like you need lots of rest and proper hydration—lots of water," the doctor explains.

Whoa, whoa, whoa, I'm thinking to myself. What does he mean, "highly stressed?" I'm stressed because I AM SICK, and no one is seeming to be able to help me get well. Yes, I'm stressed NOW because I feel AWFUL!

Mom can tell by my sunken posture and scowl on my face that his words hit me the wrong way, so she asks, "What do you mean she's stressed? Erin has been a highly active, energetic, fun-loving girl her entire life, and now she can barely get out of bed and do normal daily activities. She's been a competitive athlete and is unable to do any of those things. She's stressed because her world has crashed down on her after becoming sick. I would be stressed too if this happened to me."

Dr. Smith decides to run a few more labs (just in case) and does the standard once over, listening to my heart and lungs, checking my ears, nose, and throat, and tapping under my knees with that red-tipped metal instrument to spark a reflex response. Everything checks out normal here, and the bloodwork comes back showing some elevated numbers still consistent with this new CFS diagnosis.

"Go home and get some rest and drink lots of water," the doctor repeats again as he shakes our hand and exits the room.

What is chronic fatigue syndrome (CFS)?

Chronic fatigue syndrome (CFS) is a serious, long-term illness that affects many body systems. Another name for it is myalgic encephalomyelitis/chronic fatigue syndrome (ME/CFS). CFS can cause the inability to do usual activities, like getting out of bed. The cause of CFS is unknown but more information is coming out regularly. There may be more than one thing that causes it. It is possible that two or more triggers might work together to cause the illness. Anyone can get CFS, but it is most common in people between 40 and 60 years old. Adult women have it more often than adult men. Whites are more likely than other races to get a diagnosis of CFS, but many people with CFS have not been diagnosed with it (www.medlineplus.com).

CFS symptoms can include:

- Severe fatigue that is not improved by rest
- Sleep problems
- Post-exertional malaise (PEM), where your symptoms get worse after any physical or mental activity
- Problems with thinking and concentrating
- Pain
- Dizziness

CFS can be unpredictable. Symptoms may come and go. They may change over time–sometimes they might get better, and other times they may get worse. CFS can be difficult to diagnose. There is no specific test for CFS, and other illnesses can cause similar symptoms. A health care provider must rule out other diseases before making a diagnosis of CFS. He or she will do a thorough medical exam, including:

- Asking about medical history including family medical history

- Asking about current illness, including symptoms. The doctor will want to know how often symptoms occur, the length and intensity of symptoms, and how symptoms affect normal life
- A thorough physical and mental status exam
- Blood, urine, or other tests (MedlinePlus, 2002)

I am holding back the tears, at least until I get to the car, but I want to scream at all these people and tell them they are crazy! Can't they understand what I am saying and see that I need help? Aren't doctors supposed to be able to fix this? For goodness' sake, I'm at Duke Medical Center, and this is what I get? NO answers– well, nothing worth this drive and money.

Deflated, confused, angry, overwhelmed, and sad, I sit quietly in the passenger seat on the drive home, and I cry. I don't have the energy to speak, and what would I say at this point anyway? As I stare out the window into the blurred trees near the highway's edge, my heart breaks with another unanswered prayer.

> *God, I don't understand. Why is this happening to me? I feel like I'm crazy, but I know I'm not. I don't feel good, and I need help. Please help me.*

I do the only thing I know to do in times like this, I close my eyes and declare my life verse in my head:

"Trust in the Lord and lean not on your own understanding. In all your ways acknowledge him, and he will make your path straight. Do not be wise in your own eyes; fear the Lord and turn away from evil. This will bring health to your body and nourishment to your bones" (Proverbs 3:5-8).

Tomorrow is going to be a better day......it has to be.

Chapter 2

"*That Girl*"

◇◇◇◇◇◇◇◇◇◇◇◇◇◇◇◇◇◇◇

To understand the way forward, I return to my roots where I spent much of my childhood moving to different cities between Michigan and Ohio before locating permanently to Greenville, South Carolina. I was born in Muskegon, Michigan on April 7, 1969, the middle of three girls. My home life was blessed with loving parents who sacrificially gave to us as well as to our community. My parents held traditional family roles with my dad working as the primary breadwinner. To advance in management in the trucking industry, he was transferred regularly which meant our family moved a lot—exactly 10 times. Work took him away from our family most weekdays, so my mom was the one taking care of three very active girls. She spent many hours in our white station wagon driving us to school and from one practice or event to another. It's safe to say that our second home was on wheels. It worked seamlessly for everyone as this was our normal, and minus the typical family "stuff," our home thrived as a space filled with peace.

We were a family of faith who attended church regularly and were active in our Christian walk. We had just as many struggles as other families, but we didn't go around publicizing them or complaining to others as many did. We kept things private and dealt with life as it came. People regularly commented that we were "the perfect family" because it looked that way on the outside. This was an image that regularly followed us whether we wanted it to or not.

Growing up, I never knew a day without Jesus. I personally accepted him as my Savior at the tenderhearted age of nine. I don't remember much about that day except being in my bedroom and getting down on my knees and inviting Him into my heart. I had a solid foundation of biblical truth and knew how much He loved me and that there was a future life in Heaven awaiting me where I could live with Him forever when I left this Earth. That was for me!

Moving so often impacted me greatly, especially when I had to leave behind my very best friend of seven years. She and I were like soul sisters spending long summer days going between her house and mine. We were inseparable and being friends was easy. There wasn't drama or any strife, and that's the environment where I thrived.

During elementary school in Cincinnati, Ohio, I first discovered my love of soccer and quickly became the player who coaches noticed. I had one coach who treated me like I was an Olympic athlete and expected me to do everything perfectly for the team. I was only around nine years old, but having a strong type A personality, I rose to that level of expectation. I found myself continually in the role of leadership and was willing to partner with that pressure.

My love of the outdoors and sports came from parents who also were outdoor enthusiasts. My dad was a nationally-ranked handball player while my mom became a talented runner in her 30s. My sisters also were very active in running and sports, so much of our time was spent on a field, court, or some outdoor space.

After moving away from my best friend, the stress of having to make new friends in new environments and attending three different middle schools and two different high schools began to take its toll on me. I remember being in eighth grade coming into the school year late once again and finding myself 80 pages behind the other students in my math class. I cried repeatedly and felt a constant pit in my gut thinking that I would never catch up. Anxiety engulfed me as I feared going to school every day, being behind in my work, and never catching up. Settling for average was not my style. I expected myself to make straight As and anything less wasn't good enough.

This pressure I put on myself to be "perfect" continued, not only throughout my schooling but into my sports life as well. When we moved to Toledo, Ohio, there didn't seem to be a strong soccer program for females. My mother saw an advertisement in the local newspaper for tryouts for this select, travel soccer team and encouraged me to participate. Once we called to get specific details about the program, we learned that it was a boys' team, but anyone was invited and encouraged to try out.

"Erin," my mom said, "you need to go and try out because your dad and I believe that you will make the team."

"I can't be the only girl trying out for a boys' team," I replied just thinking about this scenario.

"Why don't you call your friend Heidi and ask her to go with you, so you aren't the only girl?" Mom confidently responded.

I gave it some thought and decided to call my friend, and to my surprise, she agreed to go to try-outs with me. I was absolutely petrified at taking that bold step, but I knew in my heart that I had to do it, afraid. We all feel fear at times, but we must stop running from things we fear; we need to step out against fear, accepting that we can't allow feelings to dictate our decisions.

Heidi and I showed up and were the only two girls there. I wanted to leave, but my mom coerced me to stay. I survived the multiple days of try-outs and grew more happy, confident, and comfortable as time went on. As a player, I believed my skills were as good as or better than many of those 90 +male players that showed up. But what chance did I really have because of my gender? This was a male team that played in a male league, and no one at this time had females on their squad. The announcement of the two team rosters—The A team which was the highest level one like high school varsity followed by the B team which was like junior varsity—came one Sunday afternoon. As I sat on the bleachers with my mom and Heidi looking poised and controlled, the nerves inside were unbridled. I thought maybe the coach who seemed to really like me might feel sorry for me enough to put me on the "B" team, but I had no expectation of making the "A" team. The names were read aloud, and I sat out of duty and respect for my fellow athletes. The "B" team names were read and neither Heidi nor I heard our name called. I resigned myself to accepting defeat when names were called for the "A" team, and toward the middle of the list, I heard my name announced. Both shock and excitement filled my body, and then came sorrow for Heidi who didn't make either team. She was a great sport and said her only reason for coming to try out was to support me.

My days as a Pacesetter soccer player continued for several years, and they were some of the best times of my life. I learned about dedication, commitment, hard work, and proving my worth to a culture that often dismissed females as a weaker vessel when it came to athletic competition. I became known throughout the organization as "that girl" as coaches and parents relentlessly yelled, "Get that girl!" I guess they thought every time our team showed up with me, a girl, on it, I wouldn't be very good and, therefore, riding the bench most of the time. Once they saw I had a starting position, the hesitation of treating me as an unequal disappeared. I played like the guys and was treated as one of them, and I thrived on the challenges this life season brought to my life.

I was also asked during this time, at the mere age of 14, by my club organization's president to head coach the U9 team that my younger sister played on. I discovered a newfound passion and talent for coaching and loved leading these girls into a deeper knowledge of the game and themselves. But, as much as I loved being the only girl on a boys' team and coaching these young players, it was an ongoing stressor in my life. I felt the continual need to prove my worth as an equal player and coach and not be judged by my gender or age. This took place every practice and every game, and we played A LOT! In one month's time, it wasn't uncommon to only have a couple of days off. Even though I outwardly flourished in this environment of high competition, the internal burden of perfectionism and performance encumbered me. This internal strife would follow me many days of my life despite my best attempts at "letting go and letting God."

Our family's final move came in 1985 to South Carolina during my sophomore year of high school. Once again, I found myself stepping into the unfamiliar with a school year that had already begun. Despite being a natural extrovert, the process of building new friendships with girls and their established "cliques" was exhausting and difficult. There were many times that I desired to shrink back and simply blend in with the masses but that wasn't possible if I wanted friendships and school involvement.

Presenting myself in a favorable light was repeatedly wearing me out. I felt like I was running for another campaign and had to "sell myself" in five minutes or less. I felt like I was giving my autobiography repeatedly to others in hopes they would welcome me into their tribe. Was a strong confident person good enough for their group? Many people didn't receive that very well, and I felt judged a lot of the time. Friends I would make often told me later that they thought I was snotty and stuck up when they first saw me, and then they got to know me and found out what a nice and kind person I was. I realized later in my life that this followed me and continues to follow me today. When a person presents themself in a confident, strong manner, oftentimes others judge them unfairly out of the insecurity and weakness it reveals within their own soul. I loved being alone as I was confident in who I was, but I also blossomed in the company of others and needed a dependable social circle. I found myself regularly being around like-minded people who had similar Christian values, worked hard in school to get good grades, and played sports. I wasn't at this new school very long before I became part of the varsity soccer team while continuing my select playing status with the area travel program. I also began teaching group fitness classes at the YMCA. Between taking an honors advanced course load, teaching group exercise fitness, and playing high level soccer, running with the cross-country team became part of the new assigned conditioning program and added more demands to my already busy schedule. Multiple colleges had already reached out regarding playing soccer for their school, including sending me letters of intent to sign once I entered my senior year. I had it all planned out, down to the top school choices including my first pick, Erskine College, which was known for its outstanding women's soccer program.

Running was a part of my life for as long as I can remember. Being a competitive soccer player demanded it, and the convenience of throwing on a pair of shoes and going out for a run was readily available in every new town I was in. I wouldn't say I loved running for the sake of running itself (actually, I quite despised it), but instead, for the outlet it provided. I got side stitches regularly, sweated profusely, and felt fatigued more times than not, but it was as much a part of my life as breathing, so I carried on. My parents ran. My sisters ran. We all ran. It was something I tolerated so that I could keep my edge in soccer and give my soul an escape from the daily pressures of my life.

One fall day during my junior year of high school, I came back from a run feeling more depleted than usual. My legs were so weak that standing up was difficult. I started having sharp pains in my abdominal area along with strong headaches and a deep sore throat. At first, we thought I was coming down with the familiar cold or flu but, quickly, the intensity of these symptoms heightened, and I needed to see a doctor. He noted my spleen was enlarged and my lymph nodes were swollen. I was diagnosed with mononucleosis, a contagious infection among teenagers and young adults. It was one of the worst cases my physician had seen.

People with mono experience extreme fatigue and body aches accompanied with fever and chills. My white blood cell count elevated to such high numbers that the doctor repeated the CBC again to confirm its accuracy. The CBC is merely a "Complete Blood Count" that shows all the basic blood tests in one panel. Upon further investigation, doctors discovered that I also had the Epstein-Barr Virus. This caused my spleen enlargement and neurological symptoms. Not much was known at the time about EBV except that it was the virus that caused mono. Most people who contracted mono didn't present with any additional symptoms from the Epstein-Barr Virus, but unfortunately, I did. All I knew was that I went from being an active person to now one that could barely move, and it scared me to death! My doctors basically told me to rest, drink lots of fluids, and avoid stress.

The days that followed proved challenging and painful. I had to temporarily withdraw from school and be put on a homebound program where one of the teachers visited my home weekly. I missed a total of 80 days of school, and most of that time was spent in bed trying to recover from flu-like symptoms. Even though my teacher, Mrs. Baker, brought assignments to me, I had to teach myself the course work, and new levels of inner chaos set in.

I remember one day sitting at my desk staring at a trigonometry test and not knowing how to answer any one of the 25 problems. My brain felt like scrambled eggs, and formulating a thought made it hurt even more. My energy was so depleted that simply sitting in the wooden desk chair seemed a task too overwhelming to bear. Tears began to flow, and I couldn't stop them. I didn't like crying in front of other people, but I felt human, and it hurt. I was vulnerable and weak, and that wasn't the image of strength that I was used to showing. How was I supposed to pass this test when I literally was struggling to hold myself up in the chair and keep from crying?

I felt I was in this place where walls were closing in on me, and there was nothing I could do to stop it. The spot where you want to yell at the top of your lungs, "I QUIT!" and run like Elijah to hide out under a broom tree. But, in that moment where human effort falls flat, the invitation for the Holy Spirit to engage is awakened. I was at the end of my capabilities, and all I knew to do at this point was seek God for help and hope He would show up in a big way!

Dear God, I whispered in my thoughts. What is wrong with me? I can't figure out one of these problems, and how am I going to pass this? I feel SO sick,

and I don't know what to do. I don't want to fail.
Please help me.

I passed that junior year and pressed on to graduate high school, maintaining my high GPA and diligently working to re-establish myself as a competitive athlete, but I was never able to sustain the level of conditioning that I had before I got sick. I was asked to be a kicker for our varsity football team my senior year, but my parents thought that was too dangerous for me to be on the field with a bunch of strong, burly guys wearing helmets and pads. College soccer was now out at least on a varsity scholarship level, and my best hope was to play intramurals. The extreme fatigue, dizziness, headaches, confusion, neurological weakness, body aches, and intestinal problems that perpetuated depression and anxiety continued. I couldn't seem to shake it no matter the amount of rest, water, good nutrition, and avoidance of stress I tried. To everyone looking on, I appeared a typical All-American teenage girl but inside I was hanging on for dear life in my new world of disorder. I was determined not to let this illness take me down and cause me to be a spectator in my own life. Surely, this wasn't the plan that God had for me.

"I want to know Christ and the power of his resurrection and the fellowship of sharing in his sufferings, becoming like him in his death, and so, somehow, to attain to the resurrection from the dead. Not that I have already obtained all this, or have already been made perfect, but I press on to take hold of that for which Christ Jesus took hold of me. Brothers, I do not consider myself yet to have taken hold of it. But one thing I do, forgetting what is behind and straining toward what is ahead, I press on toward the goal to win the prize for which God has called me heavenward in Christ Jesus" (Philippians 3:10-14).

Chapter 3

Got Grit

◇◇◇◇◇◇◇◇◇◇◇◇◇

My first attempt at college came at Presbyterian College right out of high school. I was trying to play intramural soccer, run, teach aerobics for the college baseball team, and live the normal college campus life when my medical condition worsened. I found myself making weekly trips to the infirmary. Apparently, only "really" sick people run a fever, and I never had one. I looked fine so it seemed as if people were not listening to what I was saying but instead judging me based on my appearance and my abilities inside the classroom and outside on the soccer field.

Why can't I get a high fever or break out into an awful rash or something painful so that people will believe me? I would constantly think. I even begged God for that. Living with invisible illness is painful on so many levels.

My parents were transferred back to Ohio and moved the day they dropped me off. The challenge of a new environment with this ongoing, still unresolved health crisis reached epic proportions. I was too ill to continue at Presbyterian College, so plans were made for me to return home. A wheelchair was needed to transport me through the airport as I was too weak to walk. It was a very low point in my life. Because these college plans were diverted, I investigated what I could do in town and found a small local community college to attend until I could transfer back to a four-year university. I went to school for a year with my mother.

21

That was not in my original plan, but we shared some great times, and it was comforting to have her there with me. My symptoms continued daily, and I worked to manage them at a level that I could push through. My new normal was sadly turning into disease management, but I continued to pray daily for a miracle and believed in my heart that this would turn a corner any minute. I was not going to accept this as my life. In the meantime, I had to keep going with what I had and what I knew and that was finishing college.

It was easier being at home where I had the physical, mental, and emotional support of my parents. My meals could be managed more easily with my mom cooking and my having access to the kitchen 24/7. Being in my own room was also soothing and provided needed stress relief. Having my dogs there too gave me happiness. Even though we were now in a new home and city again, all the familiarities of family were around me, and that was uplifting!

I finished my year at Davis College but lacked several credits to stay on track for graduation. Summer school at the University of Toledo met that need, and days followed with better health. My heart longed to be back in South Carolina, so when opportunity presented itself, I returned. Converse College had everything I needed to finish out my major and provided convenience to my current apartment. God always seems to know what's best for me even when it's not on my radar.

It's 5:50 pm, and I quickly park my 1985 avocado green Honda Accord. I'm always one to be on time, which, for me, means 5-10 minutes before the official start time. I need a few minutes to gather my things and get myself settled without having that rushed feeling of running late. My friend Jan decided to come along tonight so I would not be alone. We figure we would be out of here in two hours or less.

At first glance, the room appears to be full of married couples, and I feel awkward and out of place already. I'm 22 years old and don't have experience with sharing my life history nor do I really want to. I'm only here because my doctor told me this may help in dealing with my chronic illness. The church gymnasium is only 10 minutes from my college apartment. It is dark and depressing, and I'm already feeling anxious without having this environment add to the stress. I can't believe I am wasting my Tuesday night to sit and listen to people complain about their problems! I could be back at home tying up loose ends for my upcoming graduation instead of listening to this crazy advice of my college's infirmary doctor, and now I'm mad at myself. The butterflies are taking flight again as I proceed through the dark gymnasium door, and I want to turn around and run when the lady who apparently is in charge signals me to come over and take a seat. Her name tag reads, "Suzanne" and my middle name is "Susanne," so I assume this is a God sign, and I need to stay. She looks to be in her 60s, but what do I know because everyone here looks old and depressed. She's slightly overweight with silver gray shoulder length hair and speaks in such a soft tone that it's hard for me to hear.

"Hello," she says in welcoming me to the chronic fatigue syndrome (CFS) support group. "We're glad you're here. What's your name, and who is this that you brought along with you?"

"Erin," I replied, leaning in closer to hear her more effectively, "and this is my friend Jan."

"It's nice to meet you both," Suzanne responds and points to an area where we can sit down. "The meeting is about to get started so make yourselves comfortable and feel free to speak up anytime you wish and add to the conversation. This group regularly meets every Tuesday night from 6:00-8:00 pm, and we would love for you to continue joining us for future meetings."

"Thanks," I answer with a slight annoyance in my voice, though not in any way directed at her but simply at the situation in general, and we take a seat.

I glance around the room at about 30 people and quickly realize I am the youngest one in the group. The median age seems to be around 55. I don't belong here. Yes, I'm still struggling after five years of first contracting mono in high school and becoming ill with CFS, but, somehow, I'm making it all work.

Time passes and the meeting adjourns. I am relieved. I am tired of hearing the whining and complaining about how bad they feel and all the problems they live with. Most of these people got sick over 30 years ago, they never held down a job, and they still don't. Jan and I sat quietly the entire two hours not saying one word. I am not comfortable talking about my problems and listening to myself whine and complain. Yes, it's awful but these people are strangers, and they don't need to know how badly I'm suffering. I want to leave and never come back.

The clock strikes 7:58 pm, and Suzanne announces the close of the meeting. I look at Jan and nod my head as if to quickly dismiss us both before anyone tries to stop and talk to us. As I gather up my belongings, one thing being a notepad, I realize I spent the entire time thinking about getting out of here and not taking one single note. Nothing!

Jan and I both get in the car before uttering a word. She looks at me with a serious glance and says,

"So, what did you think?"

"I am not these people, and this is not my life," I boldly declare. "It will never be my life, and I will never step foot in one of these meetings ever again!"

And, with that, we leave.

I am at Converse College now in my senior year and about to graduate on May 3rd, 1991. I am living with my older sister in an apartment off campus on special permission via my family physician so that I can prepare my own food. The school cafeteria's food choices are not conducive to my allergies and restricted diet.

This is the fourth college that I have attended and not because of anything I planned. It's hard to keep going by trusting God to pull me through. But so far, I am making it work and am set to graduate on time. I am graduating with honors, which is a miracle since my struggles mentally and physically have been daunting. I keep taking the next small step, and it leads to the next one. Keeping eyes fixed on trouble leads to thoughts and behavior that are contrary to the righteousness of God. Eyes fixed on Jesus keeps our mind free of the worry and "what ifs?" I find that if I dwell on my problems, it creates high levels of anxiety and fear, so I quickly shut it down and leave it with God.

> "For God has not given us a spirit of fear (timidity), but a spirit of power, love and a sound mind" (2 Timothy 1:7).

Chapter 4

My Tribe

<><><><><><><><><><><>

Luke and I met on a blind date over the telephone. I was told that he was sort of shy, but that first phone call proved otherwise as we talked for over three hours. My guess is it was me doing most of the talking. He was six years older than me which was perfect because so many of the guys around my age of 22 were very immature. I was doing my student teaching in Spartanburg, South Carolina, and living in the home of my dad's former business secretary. She is the one who arranged a time to introduce and connect us over the telephone; cell phones didn't exist back then. My dad hired Luke straight from the Citadel along with 10 other guys from his graduating class of 1985. He loves hiring employees from this college due to its stellar reputation as a military school. Hard work, ethics, and determination are key components he looks for, and the Citadel produces these types of men. Luke certainly fits into that mold, and we connected instantly. He comes from the same line of work as my father and even drove the same company car, so the familiarity eased a lot of tension otherwise caused from being set up on a blind date.

Our first date was at McGuffey's Restaurant, and I wasn't going to order the steak unless he did so I wouldn't look high maintenance with expensive taste; my parents taught me that mannerism, and it's served me well. Luke ordered the steak, and I was so happy because that was what I really wanted too.

Conversation was fluid as we shared personal stories of similar value systems and likes and dislikes. We found quickly that we had so many things in common, and I loved the ease of being with him. He grew up in the Charleston area living only two blocks from the beach and spent much of his childhood in the ocean on a surfboard. As I spent my childhood moving from place to place, Luke was born and raised in the same home. Our lifestyles in that way were completely different, but we both grew up playing sports and loving to be active and outdoors. I didn't tell him detailed information about my health situation because it was too complicated, and I still didn't really understand it myself so why confuse and burden him with it too? I was sure that it would go away at any time so why bring it up? We entered into our marriage with me still having these pesky ongoing challenges, and we addressed them superficially as they came. I became a master at hiding my reality and trusting that God was doing something behind the scenes to fix it. It is my way of survival. I believe in the power of prayer and continued talking to God about how much I longed for a healthy body to return. God isn't looking for a huge leap. He is looking for movement.

Why God, is this happening to me? What did I do to deserve this? I feel like I'm being picked on. Do you hate me? It feels like it. So many people are doing bad things and don't know You and spend time with You like I do, so how is this fair? I don't know if I can have a family one day and work and do the things like normal people can. I want to be normal. How can I be normal when these headaches, body aches, fatigue, chronic infections, and awful allergies keep me from feeling well enough to live life? I feel like a

fake. The people at the support group said in so many
words that I would never be able to keep a job or
have a family. I don't believe them because it's not me.

Luke also is the middle child between two sisters, and we both like to claim that position as being "the favorite!" His parents, like mine, were still married to one another after 30+ years, and I liked that display of commitment that I also admired in mine. Love is a decision and not a feeling. I knew that night at McGuffey's that Luke was the man God had ordained for me to marry one day. Our Christian backgrounds were different, though, as he was brought up in the Catholic faith, and I was concerned that this could possibly bring unwanted struggles. My faith and relationship with Jesus were my number one priority, and I had to be sure that we would be able to build a solid marriage being equally yoked, meaning that we were on the same page spiritually. We went to premarital counseling, and I sought out further wisdom from older, highly valued, respected Christians in my family, and I received the peace I needed. I knew I was in love, but I needed the assurance of God's blessing over us. Our love grew, and two years later on April 3, 1993, we were married.

Our family blossomed quickly from two to five in a matter of nine years, and I was over the moon to be a mom. Many friends my age didn't desire to be a mother full time, but my heart longed for that gift and honor. I placed a high value on motherhood. Luke and I both believed in traditional roles like our parents held, so we decided that he would be the primary provider financially for our family while I stayed home and took care of the kids. I had worked several different full-time jobs in teaching and business before the kids came and continued teaching weekly fitness classes. I wanted to have my own "fun money" and time away from kids doing what I loved and believed God wanted me to do. Purpose was very important to me, and I wanted to keep my individual identity growing too.

Our daughter arrived just 13 months after we got married and on Mother's Day no less! I didn't anticipate getting pregnant so soon, but it turned out to be a double blessing! She was a beautifully packaged, healthy little girl who took my breath away and taught my heart to beat stronger than it ever had before. If I didn't know any better, I'd say her angel wings connected to my heart strings that May 8th day and caused a love explosion that forever changed my life. Kids do that, don't they? I still couldn't believe that God allowed me to be a mother, and His timing was perfect!

Next came our first son who was born 2 years and 3 months after our daughter. He, too, entered the world robust and healthy, though we quickly learned that he, at 5 weeks of age, had a severe case of reflux and colic. This lasted eleven months, 3 weeks, and 2 days. I know the exact number because I counted down the days to his one-year birthday when the radiologist who diagnosed him told me that he would be cured. We celebrated with real ponies and farm animals and 85 people at our house on August 24, 1997, because I survived! Yes, it was his first birthday, but I'll be honest in saying that the party was all about me! I made it. I survived the constant screaming and crying, no consecutive sleep for more than three hours at a time, and endless projectile vomiting. I ran into the radiologist 12 years after the diagnosis, and he told me it was the worst case of reflux he had seen to date. Tears filled my eyes at the remembrance of the pain, and I choked back the tears.

"Why didn't you tell me it would be that bad?" I asked.

"Would it have helped?" he replied.

"I guess not," I responded and stored those memories back away as another mountain God had given me to conquer. And I did.

As my health grew worse during that time of added struggle, I prayed for God to give me the strength and courage I needed to fight those daily battles. I endured the symptoms and managed as best as I could, continually asking God to open new doors of answers and solutions. My chronic fatigue syndrome diagnosis had now expanded to include fibromyalgia, migraines, chronic GI infections, interstitial cystitis (IC), Raynaud's syndrome, irritable bowel syndrome (IBS), POTS, and severe pollen related and environmental allergies.

I grew more angry, conflicted, and fearful and felt like I wasn't getting the help I needed from Luke. I pushed these feelings down inside because I didn't know how to really process them, and, honestly, I was too busy doing life to deal with it. Being a mom requires a lot, and I was sure it would all go away and was counting on God to make that happen. I also was having regular back pain that radiated nerve pain down both hips and legs and had to see a chiropractor and acupuncturist on a regular basis. On top of that, I went to other natural practitioners to keep my CFS symptoms in check to the point of management, but I had so many different diagnoses that the bottom line was: something in me was messed up. I didn't take pain medication because I didn't believe in going down that path, so I relied on natural solutions. Even over the counter medications made my body feel weird, and it wasn't worth the tradeoff.

I was taking upwards of 15 supplements a day, drinking protein powder in shakes, eating as healthily as I could manage to cook, drinking 10-12 glasses of water a day, taking cat naps any chance I could get, and begging God to fix this. It was an hour-by-hour process, and I struggled to find any real happiness. Happiness is based on circumstances, while joy is anchored in Christ. It's hard to be happy when you are in constant pain, but

I felt joyful. To others looking in, I seemed to have it all together including being the picture-perfect poster girl of health. Little did they know the battles I was fighting within.

I was on a continuum of fear, anxiety, frustration, anger, happiness, and hope. My emotions were like popcorn in a fryer– all over the place. God was my go-to helper to get me through another day. He would open doors to another doctor or "fix," and I did my best to stay in step with Him. It was a roller coaster of managing and juggling illness and life. My goal was to keep ahead of the problems, and regrouping was my middle name.

I adored my kids more than anything on this planet, and I spent lots of quality time with them. They motivated me to keep going when I wanted to quit. You can't give up when people are depending on you, but most days I was so overwhelmed that I wished I could. In life, we must REFUSE to give up. You must decide ahead of time. Colossians 3:2 tells us to "set our minds and keep it set." My will to overcome exceeded my fleshly desire to give up. I was determined to do life well and to do it at a high level. I felt physically swallowed up in a dark hole, but I believed tomorrow would be better. It had to be.

Luke started a new job, so the responsibilities of taking care of both kids primarily fell on me. I went to bed mad most every night because I felt buried under the weight of doing so much of this alone. Anger began breeding resentment, and it became my song and dance of taking it to God then picking it all back up again. I continued working part-time in my business education role, and I loved it! I also taught on average 8-10 challenging group fitness classes a week, and I loved that too. I needed this physical outlet, even though it drained me. I gave everything I had to my students, and the returned blessing kept me coming back for more. I remember, while teaching, having episodes of feeling like I was going to pass out; throughout the hour class, I would have five second episodes of seeing black. It was scary, but I began adapting to this "new normal" while always believing that it would end somehow.

Five years passed, and I began re-emerging from the dark after difficult years of balancing my health and that of my second born. Luke and I wanted three children, and I knew it was time to seek God for this other family gift. We had our second son in 2002, eight years after our daughter. He, too, was born healthy and beautiful at nine pounds. I was induced because of some medical problems while pregnant. I had separated ribs and seven bladder infections. I share the details only to show that my health had not recovered, but I struggled through. I stopped teaching aerobics at six and a half months pregnant this time. With the other two, I taught right up to giving birth. The great part about being a fitness instructor was that the actual birthing part was quick and easy, only pushing for 10-15 minutes. My obstetrician and I attributed that to strong abdominals!

I loved having three kids, and, thankfully, this third child was a breeze. He spent most of his life in a car seat, being handed off to another parent or on a soccer field as I coached the older two kids' soccer team and volunteered in their classrooms, swim team, and any other positions that needed to be filled. We were an active bunch, and I spent my days creating wonderful moments with my children. But, inside, I did everything possible simply to keep it together. The kids continued to be the pulse I needed to be the best that I could be.

Sixteen years after first becoming ill, my health crisis continued, and I ran on autopilot most of the time. Now, I had added chronic sinus infections to the mix and took 8-10 antibiotics yearly for me to continue doing the life that was set before me. Every day seemed to be met with brain fog, dizziness, aches and pains all over, and I hated taking this medicine, but I tried everything natural to heal from these chronic allergies that made it challenging to go outside. I saw an allergist for weekly immunotherapy, used OTC allergy medicines and sprays, took herbs like alfalfa, oregano, and parsley, drank aloe vera juice daily, continued my supplements and daily vitamins and minerals, drank electrolytes, and took probiotics. I managed the illness while dreaming of health. My gut reached epic proportions of pain, and it was a daily test of managing symptoms. Though I struggled with separated ribs, chronic UTI's, and back-related pain during my pregnancies, my allergies almost became non-existent. It was like living a DREAM! If only, I told my doctors, I could keep this state without being pregnant forever. My prayer life ramped up, but no breakthroughs came.

What am I doing wrong? Why is this still happening to me? I am trying to be a good wife and mom, but all of this feels like it's holding me back. I don't know what else to do. People see me and think I am the perfect picture of health. I feel like an imposter. But am I really? I really do feel joyful even though I'm angry. I feel happy at the same time I'm sad. Is it possible that these feelings can coexist? Where is my husband helping me when I need extra help? I know he has a new job, but he's still out doing his running, biking, and swimming with his buddies, and this is time he could be helping me. I know he has his own life, but I need help. I feel like I am drowning and doing everything I can to simply stay alive. I want to be a good wife, but I don't have any energy left after my responsibilities with the kids, dogs, house, and my job, to spend it on Luke. Doesn't he see that I'm suffering or am I doing too good of a job hiding it? I can't figure out how to be needy and strong at the same time. How do I express my pain without complaining? I want to quit, but I can't. I know tomorrow will be better. I learned a new acronym I like for "Hope" .... Hold On Pain Ends. OK, God, I don't understand this, but You are all I have, and I am choosing to trust You to show me the way. Jesus, You walked through the troubled waters with me as You said You would. You're the only one who understands me. Help me not lose hope.

Being a busy mom of three young kids didn't leave me a lot of time to spend alone with God, but I made it a point to at least spend five minutes here or there whenever I could. One of the best things I did was to carve out early Sunday morning runs. That time was precious to me, and I protected it at all costs. No matter how badly I felt, I always felt better after time spent with Jesus in my running shoes. I called it my "Sunday Sunrise Jesus Run." Sometimes, I listened to music while other times I ran in the silence of my own thoughts talking with and listening to God. I loved the stillness of the early morning. The geese and ducks swam beautifully in the lake or took flight overhead. I cried openly and talked to God about my hopes, dreams, discouragements, and fears as I ran down the oak tree lined streets. I loved circling the mile long lake and noticing the calm of the water. It reminded me to seek to live in peace and without strife. I had so much internal conflict that I desperately wanted to surrender. I felt God's presence so deeply here.

Distractions keep us from hearing His voice. We must be still and small as opposed to big and busy. This was my time set apart to release physical endorphins as well and receive therapy for my soul. I remember leaving the parking lot more times than not feeling more encouraged and peaceful though my physical body felt beat up and worn. Having a load to carry is not the problem. It's the way that we carry it that sets us up for failure or success. Running became the vehicle for exchanging my burdens for His peace.

Matthew 11:28 says, "Come to me, all you who are weary and burdened, and I will give you rest. Take my yoke upon you and learn from me, for I am gentle and humble in heart, and you will find rest for your souls. For my yoke is easy and my burden is light."

Chapter 5

Staring Down Goliath

Our flight to Tampa, Florida, is scheduled to leave in four hours, and I'm not sure how I'm going to be able to get on the plane with all the GI distress I am experiencing. Hurting so badly, I feel like I'm getting sick on top of my usual illness. It's hard for me to know anymore what's causing my problems. I quickly drive to the local grocery store to grab a couple bottles of Pedialyte. Surely, I can guzzle some of this down and be fine. I'm desperate, and I'm positive I'm not sick anyways. It's just my usual stuff and probably nerves on top of it.

The drive to the airport is 10 minutes, but it feels like seconds. I'm already missing my three kids, now 5, 11 and 13 years old. I'm so glad that my parents can watch them. And my in-laws are also going to come up for a couple of days, so the kids will have a great time with their grandparents. They love getting to stay up later than usual and eat all the unhealthy junk that I don't buy. Time with grandparents is a treasured gift.

We find our parking spot and begin the two-minute walk to the airport. Thank goodness for suitcases with wheels! I'm taking as much as I can fit into my large blue suitcase. Luke takes the essentials of running gear and daily wear, but I like to be prepared for all different types of weather and situations. I'm a thorough packer, perhaps an over packer, but I like to consider myself ready to deal with anything. The weight limit of each bag is 50 pounds, and mine is always one to three pounds over. I'm the one stepping over to the side of the ticket line and pulling out the heaviest things to put into my travel companion's suitcase. And then, I squeak by at 49.9 pounds, and I wonder why I am already sweating before leaving the check-in area.

Today, my heart is racing, my body is weak, and I find myself in the same position I'm always in. I feel like I can't do this plane ride alone, but I ask God to give me strength to do it anyway, and He does. I'm so nervous, but I have peace that I am doing what God wants, and that He is the one who ultimately opened this door. I wish I could stay home, but I don't have a choice. My back now requires surgical intervention after 12 years of failed attempts to achieve wellness through physical therapy, active release, chiropractic care, steroid injections, stretching, regular exercise, massage, acupuncture, heating pads/ice, magnets, tens units, support wraps, rest, natural supplements, and creams. I chose Tampa because this place is supposed to provide the least invasive, best endoscopic procedure available for my problems with my lower back. It's the area called the lower lumbar spine, L4/5-S1. My physical therapist, who is a friend and fellow athlete, recommended this place as a viable option. I saw multiple neurosurgeons and orthopedic doctors here in my hometown, but I didn't agree with the type of surgery they offered me, so I took this opportunity when it became available. For 12 years, I suffered with sciatica–an entrapped nerve sending pain down the back of my leg including neuropathy from my lower back down the legs and into my feet. I also feel tightness and stiffness constantly in my lower back like I have several 2 x 4s in there. It's hard to bend over and stand back up. Some days, it's more tolerable than others but trying to be active with my family, do my fitness job along with running, biking, and coaching soccer, is difficult.

I am in structural pain all the time, and this is adding to my overall quandary of managing it without medication and being happy. But I refuse to take any type of pain medication because my stomach can't handle it; plus, I don't want to risk becoming addicted. I keep going because I'm afraid if I quit then I will never get started again.

Getting out of shape happens quickly, and I don't want that to happen. Why is it that getting in shape takes so much time and effort while losing fitness seems to happen so fast? It seems unjust. Won't Heaven be great where we will be in perfect shape and can eat all the good stuff without it being bad for us? I want to be free like everyone else I know, especially my husband. This isn't fair. Why am I being picked on? This must be the answer I am looking for. I can't think about this surgery failing; it's not an option.

I tell Luke how I'm feeling, and he says he's sorry, but I don't feel like he is. I really wish he could feel how I do so his words would seem more sincere. I can't blame him because he's never had to go through any of this, but it just feels so lonely, and it makes me mad. I want to scream and make someone listen. It's hard being married to someone who can't really relate. I ask God so many times why it must be like this. It seems like being sick is hard enough without also having to deal with a spouse who can't connect from personal experience. Going out with other couples, I merely play along like I'm healthy and well and every time I visit a doctor, he begins his questioning with, "OK, you are a healthy thirty-eight-year-old woman…."

My mom says often, "Erin, stop looking so good and acting so happy when you go to your appointments. We know how bad you are, but you look too good, and they only see what's on the outside. You need to present yourself the way you feel."

I am in no way bragging about my appearance but merely showing the conflict of how I look on the outside compared to what is taking place on the inside. It's like I am leading a double life.

"Now Boarding Flight 353 to Tampa, Florida," the lady calls over the loudspeaker.

"This is my flight," I say to Luke as I grab my black carry-on bag and pocketbook before giving him a hug and kiss goodbye. He is taking the next flight arriving at about the same time in Florida despite our having different layovers. Luke doesn't want to fly together in case our plane crashed, which would leave our young kids without both parents. I am so upset that he is not flying with me, and it's all I can do to contain my anger and frustration of what I see as a lack of faith. We are at different places in our walk with God, and it's best not to argue about it because it does no good. Continually adding my point of view only sparks another argument, and I get tired of trying to explain it in a way that he will accept. I do it anyway and realize afterwards that I should just keep my mouth shut and maintain peace. We both are stubborn and believe what we believe. I have no intention of being hurtful to my husband when I share our differences; I know he loves me very much! I think it is important to share how much the atmosphere I am living in factors into my illness and desire to get well. We have no control over a plane crashing or not, so I trust God to provide that protection.

"OK," he says as he responds with a hug and kiss back. "I love you. See you in a few hours."

Both flights land safely as I was confident they would. I'm still mad that I had to fly alone without my husband, but I lay it aside because it doesn't do me any good to dwell on it right now. I have important things to concern myself with like surgery tomorrow. We make our way to the hotel, and I notice several couples with one of the spouses wearing a black back brace with the words of the surgery center on it. They look great, and I am so encouraged by what I see. We chose this hotel because they give discounts to all patients having procedures done at the nearby spine center 10 minutes away. I still am having a lot of GI troubles and overall feeling sick. It's that achy flu-like stuff, but being the end of May, it's probably these allergy sinus infections, which is nothing unusual for me. I didn't see the need to cancel and lose out on the thousands of out-of-pocket dollars. Not much is covered by insurance, so this is a big expense and sacrifice for us. I feel guilty having to spend this kind of money. But *it's not my fault,* I repeatedly remind myself. God is allowing this for some reason, and I'm doing everything I know to do to get well. If I did something wrong, God must be punishing me. I know this isn't the truth, but it's how I feel. Feelings are fickle, real, and valid, but I can't let them dictate my actions. This is a constant tug of war.

Tuesday morning arrives, and Luke and I head to the surgery center. I am a nervous wreck, but I remain calm in my exterior. Luke tries to make small talk, but I'm not having it. I sit quietly and begin to pray, as is my custom. I wish we could pray together, but my husband isn't ready for that yet. I ask God regularly for that to come true, and I have faith that someday it will.

We arrive at a beautiful independent hospital that boasts large glass windows and shapely architecture. It covers an entire block. I'm immediately overwhelmed and scared. I prefer smaller places.

"Now I see where all our money is going," I attempt to joke.

The morning goes smoothly with getting checked in and meeting with doctors. Luke is instructed to stay in the waiting room, and it is filled with almost every seat taken. I don't want to do this alone, but the rule states that he can't come back until

I'm prepped and ready for surgery. I wonder if I'm making a mistake. What if this doesn't work and we spend all this money for nothing? The thoughts are racing through my head, and I can't seem to shut them off. My stomach pains are ramping back up, and I feel sick everywhere. I want to go home, but I can't. I listen to the doctors explain the procedure as they sort through all the paperwork.

"Do you have any questions?" the surgeon asks.

"No," I reply. And with that the nurse takes me back for prepping and brings Luke to my room for some last-minute comfort. It's so reassuring to have him here with me.

I am wheeled back to the operating room, and though some anesthesia in my IV has been administered, I am still awake. I am going in and out of hazy consciousness when suddenly I begin hearing drills and loud noises. It sounds like I am in a workshop. I don't think this is normal, so I begin talking aloud to the doctors and hear them say, "Give her some more anesthesia." I see a handful of people and a computer type screen in front of me showing what appears to be my spine. Is this really happening? Am I watching my own surgery take place? I must be dreaming.

As I lay on my stomach, I continue to hear the deafening sounds of hammers, drills, and other tools and some minimal pain in my back area. I am still going in and out of consciousness and hear the doctors repeat a few more times, "Give her some more anesthesia." At one point, I feel loopy drunk and ask the surgeons to explain on the screen what is happening.

"Be quiet and relax," one of them answers.

I am in a large recovery room of about 10 other patients and probably more, but I'm too out of it and in too much pain to count. Each room is divided by curtains on either side, and I am looking through fuzzy lenses for my husband.

"Where's Luke?" I ask the nurse who's pushing my bed.

"We will get him shortly," he replies.

Another nurse enters and now I realize that I remember most of the surgery. The net holding back my hair is soaked, and my entire head of hair is wet. It's dripping wet as if I just got out of the shower. This is not normal. I have had four surgeries prior to this one, and this has never happened before. My entire back is in excruciating pain when another nurse says, "You win the prize for the sweatiest patient we've ever had!"

That's not a prize I want to win, I thought.

The nausea heightens and vomiting begins. The total count reached 18 times. I know the precise number because I wanted to share the magnitude of this terrifying experience with my family. This cannot be good coming off back surgery. I ask for more nausea medicine, and I am told that they have given me all they have available.

Certainly, there is something they can do for me!
Where is Luke? Why haven't they brought him up
here yet to be with me? I need help. I'm really scared.

A new nurse comes by, and I signal her to come talk to me. I must get out of here. It feels like these people are trying to kill me. I need Luke.

"Can I get up and get dressed now so I can leave?" I weakly say to her.

"We can't let you leave until you stop vomiting," she answers.

"OK, then help me to the bathroom so I can get dressed," I reply.

The nurse assists me with my bag of clothes to the nearest restroom, and I determine that I am getting out of here NOW before something worse happens to me. Choking back the nausea and vomit, I somehow manage to get my clothes on and make my way outside the bathroom door where I'm instructed to be seated. Meantime, my vision is still blurred, but I can see two of the doctors that operated on me giving me dirty looks, one stating loudly in a sarcastic, mocking voice, "She had a stomach bug and didn't tell us, so it's on her."

I muster up enough energy to thwart that attack with language that isn't in my regular vocabulary but seems appropriate for this time. I am still holding back the tears and nausea so that I can be discharged. My papers are signed, and I am helped into the wheelchair, still alone without my husband. As my nurse is wheeling me down the hallway, I finally spot Luke and ask where he's been. He has no idea the ordeal I am going through, and I don't have the energy to explain it right now.

"No one came and got me," he says.

As I approach the outside of the covered pick-up area, Luke goes quickly to get the car.

> *Hold it in. Hold it in…. Hold it in! Wait until you*
> *get to the car so you can get out of here*, I am saying
> to myself.

Luke pulls the car around and as I step one foot out of the wheelchair and into the back seat, I cannot hold back the nausea any longer.

Back at the hotel, my pain is a 10 out of 10. I refuse the pain medication because after taking one, the side effects are too much for my body to handle, and I cannot deal with both problems. The night is long, and pain carries over into the next day where I try to do some walking and visit the physical therapist. I cannot stop crying and begging God to take all this away. Why are all these other people in the hotel lobby doing great, and I am suffering so badly! All the staff made this sound so easy, like it was nothing. If this is nothing, I would hate to see something! And now Luke is heading back to South Carolina to work, and I am here all alone. We thought this was going to be a breeze–a "minimally invasive surgery." Something went terribly wrong, and now I am alone in a city far from home left to have unfamiliar housekeepers change my bandages, take back the rental car, and get myself loaded onto an airplane. I cry out to God like never in my life before. *I NEED You! I cannot do this.*

I wear my favorite pale colored yellow sweater and skirt for the trip home because it's comfortable, and the yellow color reminds me of sunshine. This makes me happy wearing something cheerful, and right now I am desperate for some cheer. The black back brace with the surgery center's name printed on it is around my waist, and I feel cheated. This was supposed to be my cure. Pulling my big blue suitcase through the airport listening to the squeak of overtaxed wheels, I hide the tears. Leaning up against the windowed wall waiting for my plane to board, I meet with God like I do on a regular basis. Sorrow and pain overwhelm my soul and then that glimpse of hope returns to fill those empty places. *Hold On Pain Ends (HOPE)*, I recite repeatedly in my head. My family needs me strong, and I can do this.

"I CAN do ALL things THROUGH Christ who
gives me strength" (Philippians 4:13).

Chapter 6

Waving the White Flag

These 13 months after back surgery are proving a nightmare. I am not sure if all of it resulted from an actual failed surgery or an eruption of my autoimmune issues. Either way, it is terrible! The neuropathy extends from my head to both feet, and I feel like an electrical circuit board with mismatched wires that short circuit continuously. My coordination is bad, and I feel like I am divided up into multiple pieces instead of one fluid moving body. The pain across my lower back continues and feels very stiff. Bending over is fine but getting up is painful. I don't think staying in a forward flexion position is a good option for a near 40-year-old woman. That is for old people. Walking is painful, and my brain labors from pain. I told Luke that if this isn't multiple sclerosis then I don't know what is. Multiple sclerosis or MS is a disease that impacts the brain and spinal cord which make up the central nervous system and controls everything we do. A lot of symptoms cross over into many different categories, so it is very confusing to know which tail is wagging which dog.

This all leads to more doctor visits including a neurologist, chiropractor, sports specialist, and nutritionist. The neurologist performs nerve conduction studies and tries several steroid injections to ease my pain. Nothing helps. Frustration and disappointment consume me. White lesions symptomatic of people with MS are found on my brain MRI scan, and I'm diagnosed with "possible

MS-will continue to follow." The lesions could also be a sign of past head trauma, possibly from a major concussion I sustained in soccer as a teenager. So, no clear-cut answers come once again. I feel like I am on a never-ending hamster wheel. What good is it to "follow me" throughout upcoming years until I am so bad that I am wheelchair bound and put on regular medication to control symptoms? That is NOT an option for me.

I am too young to participate in what I feel is a medical circus. I juggle doctor visits like a clown juggling balls on a unicycle. I don't have a money tree in the yard, and Luke prefers I use our insurance. I agree, but that proves harder and harder each year as my symptoms grow, and my Western medicine doctors don't give definitive solutions other than prescribed medication. I refuse medicine that comes with a list of side effects that would add to my already long list of problems. I want to get to the root cause. Plus, my gut literally can't handle taking strong medication, so I live with the pain instead. That is a continued work in progress.

I diligently work on healing with some homeopathic practitioners as much as I can afford to. Homeopaths look at the symptoms of disease and work through natural means to help a person regain health. This is considered alternative medicine and is not covered by regular health insurance. So, this extra money comes out-of-pocket and strains the already tight budget. Luke and I disagree strongly on a regular basis over the validity and direction of my care, and I hate this as much as I do the illness. I feel I have to justify and "sell" him on every alternative idea. He is the main income earner and in charge of the major finances in our home. I agreed to that role and respected it until I didn't. The strain tests me in ways I never experienced before.

Marriage is about compromise. When spouses see things through different lenses, it leads to a fork in the road. It's at these crossroads where we make decisions. I began to feel that the Lord is intentionally allowing us to go through these circumstances to force us both to turn more to Him. The Bible says that God's thoughts and ways are above ours. I ask God to give me answers for my health, while at the same time have Luke and me more on the same page. Trusting God on this deeper level with both things takes more faith than I sometimes have.

In Romans 7 Paul says, "I do not understand what I do. For what I want to do I do not do, but what I hate I do. And if I do what I do not want to do, I agree that the law is good. As it is, it is no longer I who do it, but it is sin living in me. I know that nothing good lives in me, that is, in my sinful nature. For I have the desire to do what is good, but I cannot carry it out. For what I do is not the good I want to do; no, the evil I do not want to do-this I keep doing. Now, if I do what I do not want to do, it is no longer I who do it, but it is sin living in me that does it." Whew! That spins my head around in a bunch of circles. I feel this endless tug, and I yearn to do the right thing by God. By nature, I am a problem solver, and I feel like my health hangs in the balance daily and is dependent on that answered prayer. I hope Luke and I can include God's direction together in the search, but, sometimes, I find it easier to go alone. And so, I do. I'm repeatedly tested by "Be still and know that I am God" (Psalm 46:10).

At the rate my health is going, I believe my life is dependent on Luke seeing God's way, which inevitably is mine also. I experience deep levels of trust followed by periods of unshakeable fear. I long for the inner chaos to silence. I tell God repeatedly that I cannot handle both the ongoing health crisis as well as the marital tension. Every time God answers me with this phrase, "No you can't, but I can." Tough circumstances require deep faith and moves you either closer to God or away from God. Faith moves in tandem with patience. I want to move closer to Him and grow! The stress mounts, but I resolve to get to the root problem. After all, this is my health, and "health is wealth!"

What I call a marked moment that resonates in my spirit like no other occurs one day in June. Moments like this feel like they can knock me over with their power and awareness. If you haven't yet had one, keep practicing and seeking God. Sometimes, it requires ongoing action, so don't give up. The simplicity of spending time in His presence brings results. It goes deeper than just our mind and thoughts; it is beyond head knowledge. It's like somewhere in this deep place in our spiritual being a huge lightbulb goes off and alarms start ringing. It's a moment that demands pause. It's the coming together of revelation and wisdom that ignites a spark of change if we're willing to receive it. This morning's run is one of these marked moments.

The air is heavy as it often is in June in South Carolina, and I am determined to get outdoors to make another attempt at putting in some time in my running shoes. The trails are shaded by large trees along the 3.2 miles of winding asphalt. The creek has enough water to hear the trickle as it moves over the rocks and sand formations. The calm of the water reminds me of the verse in Psalm 23 that says, "He leads me beside quiet waters, He restores my soul." It paints an amazing picture of Jesus as our Shepherd, and I cling to this image as I run. As the shepherd guides the sheep along the still waters, Jesus leads us there when we need times of calm and refreshment. We hear Him speak when we silence the noise. Even though my allergies heighten being outdoors on the trails, I decide to suffer the physical consequences in exchange for the peace it gives my soul.

Nothing I seem to do helps take away the constant symptoms I manage, so I figure I can't stop living and will do what my mind says it enjoys. Nature is at the top of this list. Therefore, I choose to do what my spirit dictates instead of listening to my body. I learned by now that if I listen to my body, I won't do much of anything, and I can't accept that for my life. Ecclesiastes 11:4 is a great reminder that if we wait for perfect conditions then we will never get anything done. I hold this as a life mantra.

This day is no different. I struggle to regain a regular pattern and schedule of running, and it feels like it will never return the way it was before surgery. As I wrestle to maintain proper form, I begin talking to God. I hold the image of the man running aimlessly beating the air described in 1 Corinthians chapter 9. I sense this is what I look like to passersby, a body flailing in all kinds of silly directions. My ego is bruised. My body aches. My feet grow numb. And frustration envelopes my soul. I approach another runner on the trail, and I can't wait to get past him so the tears I hold back can finally flow. It is like a breached dam about to burst. As I pass the unfamiliar runner, my eyes blur as the tears fall.

God, would You just WORK WITH ME! I scream in my thoughts. Without a second's delay, I hear the still small voice of God respond,

"No, Erin. YOU work with Me!"

Stunned in my tracks, my running quickly halts as I realize the words I spoke. Matthew 12:34 says: "Out of the overflow of the heart, the mouth speaks." *What did I say?* I repeat it aloud several additional times. I question at this moment the belief system I hold based on the words that echo in my mind. I thought I trusted God to grow my faith. I thought I followed His lead and not my own. And I thought I learned the practice of letting go and resolving anger. Everything I thought was a lie but now I know the truth based on the power of my words. Ugly tears turn into full on sobbing, and I don't care at that moment if another person passes by or not. Time stands still. My knees weaken. My posture relaxes. And I raise the white flag of surrender.

This meeting happens unannounced to me. The Bible says He knows the end from the beginning, so He knew all along that it would take place. I merely showed up to run—or so I thought. Marked moments are available for all of us who live in the awareness of God's presence. When we show up, things happen. It requires a prepared "YES" in our spirit. The Bible says in Matthew 7 that the narrow gate is small and that only a few find it. It's the road that is less traveled compared to the wide gate that most take. The broad path leads to destruction because its desires are those of the world. The narrow road leads to life because it requires leaving behind more fleshly baggage to go further with God. The Holy Spirit shows me this warm June day my baggage that I need to drop to run a stronger race with Him. It's like shedding extra physical weight or unnecessary gear. It is time for me to stop trying to control situations and let Him work. Why is this so hard for me to let God be God? I say I trust God, but do my actions really align with these words? I have growing to do that's for sure, and I resolve to go the distance. Defeat only comes when we stop moving forward in the direction of our "YES!"

Chapter 7

Movement is a Gift

⬦⬦⬦⬦⬦⬦⬦⬦⬦⬦⬦⬦⬦⬦⬦⬦⬦⬦⬦⬦⬦⬦⬦⬦⬦⬦⬦⬦⬦⬦⬦⬦

In preparation for this first half marathon, I found myself in a lot of pain. Thankfully, Luke has a friend who sees a specialist chiropractor called a Non-directional Non-force Chiropractor, with great results and gave him his information. It was a long shot to get in the same day I called, but I did. I was desperate after my usual attempts at avoiding the pollen outside, trying to juggle the right amount of training with rest, avoiding unnecessary obligations to get extra rest, eating somewhat clean including drinking no coffee or other beverages besides water, and taking my natural supplements to combat the aches and pains. It's crazy the things I must do to try to keep this body up and moving, let alone arrange for racing. By the grace of God, a one-hour appointment time was available, and, of course, I dropped everything and drove the two-hour round-trip distance to Columbus, North Carolina, to see him.

Dr. Landry isn't the typical chiropractor you see weekly for quick adjustments but, instead, provides people lasting relief in as little as one to five visits. Problem solved. No need to come back. At least that's what I was told. As a first-time patient, I had a million medical questions and volumes of paperwork to fill out, giving my life history and labeling that darn outline of a man showing numbers 1-10 of my levels of pain. Pain is relative. My number three may be others' 10. At this point, just ask me what doesn't hurt and that will save a lot of time for all of us! I didn't have energy to waste on small talk because I had a race to run in the morning. So, I began the conversation with my reasons for being here:

"Dr. Landry," I said. "There are three things I need to say. First, I believe you were sent by God to help me with this pain I'm in so that I can run this half marathon tomorrow because I believe He has me doing this race for a reason. Secondly, I know that this treatment won't probably work past tomorrow and that's OK. I need to be able to run 13.1 miles and right now I can't walk past 15 minutes. And, lastly, I will gladly come back next week and pay the $85 again to redo everything I'm about to screw up."

Looking stunned but enlivened and laughing quietly with a big smile, Dr. Landry replied, "OK then. That's not much of a tall order to fill. I guess we have work to do!"

And, with that, I proceeded with my hour-long adjustment and drove back home.

Lake Greenwood is abuzz on this humid April morning as runners gather to test their fortitude in finishing this half marathon distance. This is the first time I am running 13.1 miles, and it's my first time at Lake Greenwood. I'm freaking out a little bit after the day I had yesterday not even being able to finish the 20 minutes of easy running that my training plan called for. I had to walk my way back home after about 10 minutes because my back-related nerve pain was so bad all the way down both legs and into my feet. My feet were going so numb that my brain couldn't muster up any more strength to tell them to go, so I ditched the remaining time and went home. Having raced three weeks ago, I feel my broken body screaming for a break, but I need it to cooperate this one last time. Then, a welcome reprieve is in order.

It's early Saturday morning and though the race begins at 8:00 am, Janet and I are here at 7:00 am to warm up and make our four trips through the port-a-potty line. She is proving to be my faithful training and racing buddy who pushes me to be my best. I gave her a head's up on the phone last night about what kind of shape I am in and that I wasn't sure that I could do the race.

"What are you going to do?" she asked.

"Show up and see where God leads," I reply.

"Yeah, but how are you going to run 13.1miles if you can't even walk?"

With a calm peace I wasn't accustomed to before a race, I replied, "I have absolutely no idea, but I'm going to go and see what God does. I know this sounds ludicrous, but all I know is that God told me to do this race, and that's what I'm going to do."

If God calls us into something, He is faithful to equip us with all that we need to be successful. Our role is to step out and release our faith. Logically, it makes no sense, but I can't get into reasoning. It's a sin, and it gets me all confused and off course. I know this race was ordered by God, and my job is to do what I can to prepare and trust Him with the rest. And that's what I did and what I am doing.

So here I am, sporting new hot pink knee tape because, out of nowhere, my right knee began hurting last week. Pre-race ice packs discreetly sit under the back support brace I bought in Tampa four years ago during that surgery nightmare. I look like the walking wounded and laugh along with Janet at what the other runners must be thinking. My parents just arrived to cheer me on and even Mom is asking how I am going to do this. I shrug my shoulders and confidently say once again, "In all honesty, I have absolutely no idea. I'm not trying to be a martyr or sound heroic. It's the only answer I have."

Janet is still talking smack about my convincing her to do this race with me just three weeks after our last one. I figure I'd better take it while I can because once I stop, I'm probably done. It's a smaller race with about 200 people and not super hilly, though I prefer rolling hills. I get bored with flat surfaces when I can see so far up ahead that it begins to psych me out. I think this is the distance I really want to continue running but not sure that my body is going to be able to keep up with the mileage. I guess I'll have to take it one day at a time like I have been doing and see where God takes me. Too many people think the idea of running 13.1 miles seems impossible, but I figure a word from God and a good training plan is all I need. I have both.

The male racecourse director picks up his white megaphone and gives the five-minute warning before the race begins. Mom and Dad give us both hugs and wish us a great, fun race. Janet and I make our way to the front of the pack at the Start Line because this race is a gun start which means time starts with the clock and not by an individual chip.

"So, what are you going to do?" she says.

"Here are my plans," I answer. "Since your race pace is slower than mine, I'm going to start off with you to keep my heart rate down and hope that I can run. If I can't run, then you go on ahead without me, and I will figure something out. But I don't think that's going to happen. I'll run with you the first half of the race, and then if I'm feeling good, I'll go on ahead if that's OK with you?"

"Yeah, that's fine," she responds. "But you're going to have to keep talking to me while we run so I can make it."

The clock begins the final two-minute countdown and nerves take hold, but I feel ALIVE! It's empowering to pin a race number onto my shirt; it signals my warrior spirit to awaken to the impossible. It's the love of a challenge I told God about one day as I sat with Him talking about my life. I was only a young girl of about 12 years old, but I already knew then that I thrived in the unthinkable. Easy was boring. Sometimes over these years, I did regret making that statement. I talk to God and feel His peace immediately sweep over me.

> *God, I know I can't do this, but You say that all things are possible with You and to those who believe. I believe I am here today for a reason even though I don't know what that reason is. I need You to be in every step and every breath that I take. Apart from You, I can do nothing, and this physical body is constant proof of that. I'm ready to go. Show up BIG today, please God. I can't walk, but I'm trusting You to run. Let's do this.*

The gun sounds, and we take off. One foot in front of the other, I say in my head and sure enough, I am upright and running.

"How are you doing?" Janet says smiling.

"So far, so good," I reply, and, with that, we press on through the first six miles together and talk the entire way. Janet is more labored in her breathing, so I do most of the talking but that's OK since I am used to that. The pain is still there across my lower back and there is numbness in both feet, but the rod-like pain down my legs is absent. There is pain in my hips, but it's not connecting down to my feet like it was yesterday. It's truly a miracle! It is tolerable for me and with each passing step, I feel stronger and more alive.

"At this turnaround up ahead at mile 6.5, I'm going to go on ahead if you're alright with that?" I announce to Janet. "I feel like God is giving me this ability to go, and I need to take it!"

"Sure, go," she says, "just come back and find me when you're done in case I pass out somewhere before the Finish Line."

With a chuckle, we part ways. I turn up the music in my earbuds to hear contemporary Christian music playing with lyrics that inspire and encourage me to keep running my race. As I get through miles seven, eight, and nine, I take in the stillness of the atmosphere around me. Cows are grazing in green pastures on both sides of the road, and I can smell their scent as the breeze blows forcibly by. I don't even mind the smell or the strong winds because my body can feel it, and that is a gift! If I can feel, and even though it's pain, it means that I am alive and that means that God is working! Could this wind be signaling something more prophetic? Is this representing a season of change?

My legs are loosening up now even more, and the pain is the lowest I have experienced in years. I'm not sure what is happening, but it's as if my mind has taken me to another place- a different atmosphere. My steps quicken, and my breathing deepens but the usual laboring is gone. I feel good. I am talking to God in my head as I recall this one ongoing prayer that stuck with me a few years back when I ran into Gail on my neighborhood trails.

It was soon after my back surgery four years ago, and I was struggling to run. Gail was a neighbor and acquaintance from the YMCA. She, too, had been a long-time runner before nagging injuries became too much, and she decided to quit. Then, she became a brisk walker. She told me that God took away her desire to run and that He would do the same for me. I prayed continually for that desire to leave, but it only grew stronger. Thinking I must be praying wrong, one day recently I heard in my spirit,

Erin, this is Gail's story and not yours! So, with that new revelation, I continue seeking that answer to "what is my story?"

Coming back into race mode, my watch beeps loudly signaling another mile completed. My thoughts get lost in the freedom of movement, and I want to stay here as long as I can. *Mile 11,* I say aloud to myself both shocked and excited. I cannot believe I have made it to mile 11! Instantly, I hear God say that He is giving me my running back. My favorite song, *Mountains* by Lonestar, pipes into my ears as I feel in my spirit the Lord saying *Go! Don't be scared. Don't hold back because of pain. "Soar high on wings like eagles. Run and don't grow weary" (Isaiah 40:31).*

With those truths ringing loudly in my soul, a smile so big comes across my face, and I open my stride and run faster than I ever remember running. I am hitting 7:30 minute mile paces, and I am blown away. I round the final turn coming down the home-stretch and see the Finish Line. Fans are cheering loudly, clapping, and calling out names of runners making the final stretch. Mom and Dad look as shocked as I feel that I am coming in currently, and we celebrate with hugs and congratulations!

"I need to go back and find Janet," I say quickly.

"OK, honey. Great job! We are so proud of you. We need to head out, but we will call you later," my parents respond.

"I love you both and thank you so much for cheering me on as always!" I say, and, with that, I go back to run the remaining distance with my friend. Still having energy, I catch her in the last mile and run the final one with her. Movement is a gift!

Chapter 8

Running Ahead

◇◇◇◇◇◇◇◇◇◇◇◇◇◇◇◇◇◇◇◇◇◇◇◇◇◇◇◇◇◇

Janet is known as my "BRF." BRF stands for best running friend. The acronym came a few months ago when I first met her at this incredible new gym where I began working out and teaching fitness classes. I LOVE working at this gym as it is not only beautiful, but it is also very quiet. I am completely convinced that it is a huge gift from God sent straight to me. It is a 5-10 minute walk from my youngest child's elementary school, so I can park my car in the carline early and walk over with all my gym gear. It's typical for me during these short walks to talk to God about how thankful I am for this place. Getting in the carline this early helps too because it puts me at the very front of the line so I can get my elementary school son then head straight over to the middle and high school to get my other two kids. I am all about seizing time to do my personal workouts because being a busy mom, teaching 8-10 fitness classes a week, coaching soccer, volunteering for the kids' school and activities, and all things mothering and homemaking, it can be hard to squeeze in my own fitness aside from instructing my classes. It is a lot but it's what I do and all I know. Remember—waiting for perfect conditions often means nothing gets done!

Back in February, a couple of months ago, I was recovering from another traumatic health scare. I had been doubling over in pain for months leading up to Christmas last year with, again, no clear-cut answers as to what was causing it. These pains became so sharp in my lower abdominal quadrant that it caused me to curl up in a ball and cry for hours. Because of my ongoing issues, I wasn't alarmed until it became so unbearable that I got up early enough to be at the outpatient clinic by their 6:00 am opening. As a 41-year-old woman, I didn't fit the stigma of having a gallbladder attack, so the four previous doctors had dismissed it.

"You are young and not overweight, so you don't fit into the diseased gallbladder category," they would say and turn me away. I left defeated and burdened with getting answers for this situation now too.

'Overwhelming' is a word that seems too small to capture my real feelings. But, on this one 6:00 am morning, I finally got the answers I needed. "Young lady," the doctor said, "you don't fit the typical mold for having a gallbladder problem, but tests show that is what it is."

Finally, the answers I needed! It was my gallbladder, and I was scheduled for surgery the week after Christmas. Well, as it seems to go with me, I progressively got worse to the point on Christmas Eve that I went into a full-blown attack that landed me in the hospital through Christmas Day and into the following week. Take it from me—being hospitalized over the Christmas holiday is difficult because doctors are scarce and the ones that are present appear to be mad that they are. It was four days of being moved between three different hospitals, and it was awful!

Luke drove me to the local hospital that Christmas Eve evening after I finished getting my daughter's big red velvet bow placed on her new car we were surprising her with since she now is 16 years old and can drive unrestricted. And there was writing the Santa Claus letter with my non-writing hand so as not to ruin my eight-year old's Christmas believing magic. Looking back now, it was a miracle that I survived hosting my annual brunch and getting all the pre-Christmas items in order while in excruciating pain.

As Luke and I got to the hospital, I announced, "I am going to pass out!"

"Let me park the car right over here, and we can go in," he said.

"No, I need you to drop me off now!" I pronounced with urgency and aggravation.

"Hang on, the lot is right here," he said and, with that, I demanded an expedient drop off at the hospital front doors.

Thankfully, a door man was there willing to welcome me, but there was no time for small talk. I grabbed hold of his black jacket so I wouldn't fall to the ground and signaled to the wheelchairs. Upon landing my backside in the chair, I felt my body going into a state it never had before. The energy was draining out of me, and the room was spinning more and more. I could barely hold my head up or formulate any thoughts let alone words as the registration nurse attempted to ask me the usual questions before I began losing consciousness. I was seeing more and more black but giving myself the biggest pep talk of my life.

Hold on, Erin. You can't pass out. You aren't certain that Luke will handle your medical history questions and care the way you desire. He will probably do whatever the doctors say and agree with them, and that's not what you want. Too many doctors up to this point have misdiagnosed and misinformed you, so you need to take care of it yourself. Do NOT go out. HOLD ON. Stay here. Stay here.

With that, I heard loud sirens beeping, and through my dazed and fuzzy vision, I saw nurses and doctors rushing to me in the waiting area. My buttoned-down plaid shirt was quickly torn open, and electrodes of all kinds were placed on me as they were wheeling me back to a room. There was loud chatter and calm commotion, and I remember seeing my blood pressure numbers going way down to a dangerous level.

> *Hold on, Erin. Stay awake, stay awake, stay awake. You need to take care of yourself and be alive for your daughter to get her first car tomorrow morning. It's almost Christmas and you can't die and leave your family. Don't die, don't die, don't die. Please God, let me live. I need to live. Please God, help me. It is not my time to die.*

As Believers, it's important to agree with God and work with Him on why we are going to live! We must know our assignment and bind any attempts by the Enemy to take us out before our time. Matthew 18:18 tells us that "whatever you bind on earth will be bound in heaven, and whatever you loose on earth will be loosed in heaven." The prophetic purpose is what pulls us through these ill-laden times.

The doctors stabilized me, and the days and weeks following that episode challenged me more with tolerating more pain. I had the gallbladder removed a week later because I was too weak and sick to have the actual surgery on Christmas Eve. To be honest, I don't even remember the surgery because I was a blur with exhaustion and pain like never before. And being one to enter a new year with a bang, this one in 2011 came in the form of an EMS ride to yet another hospital due to complications after surgery.

Being frail and easily winded, I needed a place to train in order to regain strength and stamina lost from the gallbladder ordeal. This new gym has been such a godsend for me to be able to work on getting my strength back and structure sound. Not only am I dealing with the mechanical problems of my body but also my inner health and healing. Levels of fatigue, weakness, and exhaustion reached new levels, and I was diagnosed again with adrenal exhaustion.

Adrenals are the little glands that sit at the top of the kidneys and filter out stress. When a person is under a large amount of stress, the adrenals can become taxed and depleted. Western medical doctors often don't recognize Adrenal Exhaustion or Adrenal Fatigue as a "real" illness, but my naturopaths do, and I lean towards believing them and following their advice. I am taking my full spectrum of natural supplements and adding electrolytes as I can tolerate. Vitamin B12 shots are also happening each week as I'm trying to get some energy and stamina back. Still, I am not able to take anything regularly for the pain, so I live with it. A lot of days, I feel like my brain literally hurts trying to handle it all. As I am in the habit of doing, I spend time with Jesus reading some devotional books and praying when I can. It's been all I can do since December to get through pedaling 30 minutes easy on a bike and most days I struggle to make it through a full shower of body washing, hair shampooing, and styling. I break it up into blocks taking needed rest breaks in between.

Again, Luke and I are at a crossroads with all of this, and I long for the day to feel like I am believed in. I continue asking God to get us both on the same page because I feel many days like a test rat caught in the middle of two disagreeing scientists. I can't seem to find the right words to explain all of this. I know what I feel and what God says to me, but I struggle relaying it effectively.

I don't even know if it's possible to put expressible words with it. I'm trying everything I believe God is showing me to do to release my faith and expect the right results. And, to those looking in, I still appear to be the picture of health with no problems at all.

"So, I say, live by the Spirit, and you will not gratify the desires of the sinful nature. For the sinful nature desires what is contrary to the Spirit, and the Spirit what is contrary to the sinful nature. They are in conflict with each other, so that you do not do what you want. But if you are led by the Spirit, you are not under law…. Since we live by the Spirit, let us keep in step with The Spirit" (Galatians 5:16-17; 25).

When February came and Janet was looking for training advice, I agreed to do some of the running with her. Since she was a beginner runner and I was trying to get my running back, I thought this was a perfect partnership. She also is a believer in Jesus, so we have that shared value system which is very important to me. It wasn't long before I knew this was another divine meeting from God! She ran a lot more slowly than I was used to running so this was perfect timing because I needed it to be slow and easy right now. She didn't know that I had been praying more boldly for the "impossible" and for opportunities to open up more to others. For several years now, I have prayed this prayer regularly. Up to this point, I didn't share much about my health because of the complexity and fear of judgment. It's easier not to have to explain it all and sound like I am complaining about a bunch of stuff. I'm routinely in a joyful state around others, so no one would believe me if I shared the truth. However, God has taught me recently that not sharing my burdens with others so that they could pray for me was ultimately denying both of us a blessing! I had always believed that it was complaining, and I didn't want to be one of those whiners. That was another one of those marked moments, I like to say. The lightbulb flipped on inside my soul. *Could it be that I believed a lie all these years? Did the Enemy sell it to me, and I bought it without thinking twice? Is there really an Enemy that the Bible talks about or is he that Halloween costume character in a red suit and black horns carrying a pitchfork?*

Allowing others to pray for us opens a window of opportunity for them to experience God. Prayer is a privilege. Denying others of this privilege is pride. Amid two or more, God says, He is there. The power of prayer moves mountains. It invites others into His presence and aligns hearts and minds with His. It is then through this communication that God's incomprehensible goodness, faithfulness, and willingness can be accomplished by way of blessings and favor.

My mindset is changing, and the running relationship with Janet is quickly becoming a great friendship. While running, we talk about our lives and that opens the door for me to begin sharing my true authentic self.

This is new for me, and it's scary. Fear will either push you away from the Lordship of Jesus or draw you closer to Him. With everything I am going through, though, it helps to talk about it with someone other than my husband. And another female unquestionably helps! I like a new sense of freedom that I haven't experienced before. Plus, I've been used to being a solo runner for most of my life, so this is a new experience as well.

I don't like being vulnerable, and it's hard for me to trust people with my deep issues. I think a lot of that has to do with moving so much and not getting much time to build meaningful relationships. Some things take time, and I didn't want to share personal things with people that I would have to say goodbye to in a couple of years. But now I am planted and eager to keep growing friendships.

I remember one run soon after Janet started following the training plan that I devised for her. It turned out to be no ordinary run. She planned to run between seven and eight miles, and I hoped to do a small part of it with her, as much as the pain and fatigue would allow.

"I'm not sure how much I can do today, but I will go as long as I can," I said to Janet upon meeting her in the gym lobby.

"OK," Janet replied. "That's fine."

We started outside around the perimeter half mile track and continued the route on the connecting church campus. It was the ideal spot for running and avoiding cars and traffic. We began talking about all things life and one mile led to another and then another. Pain seared down both legs from my back, numbness ensued, and overall feelings of "yuck" filled my body and yet my soul sang with joy and gladness.

"Let's keep going as long as you can," Janet suggested. "I think today is your day to make the whole run!"

Doubting the possibility and yet embracing the unyielding hope, I responded, "Sounds good to me, but first, since we are at the halfway mark, let's go to the bathroom and get some water. I am hurting and need to stretch a few minutes and take a little walk break." Admitting weakness is difficult for me because I'm usually in the position of leadership, and leaders need to show strength. But, with Janet, I felt like I could be myself, and I was willing to keep practicing.

God gave me the Corinthians 12:9-10 passage to declare over my life. I was speaking it regularly and writing it down on notecards in my car or in my writing journals. I felt like Paul when he said, "My grace is sufficient for you, for my power is made perfect in weakness. Therefore, I will boast all the more gladly about my weaknesses, so that Christ's power may rest on me. That is why, for Christ's sake, I delight in weaknesses, in insults, in hardships, in persecutions, in difficulties. For when I am weak, then I am strong." As my body is growing physically weaker, I am feeling deeper connections of strength in my spirit.

As I walked back outside, I heard a God whisper in my spirit, *Here it is! Take it. It is time.*

"Janet!" I exclaimed with deeper positivity and excitement, "I need to do the entire run. I know this sounds crazy, but I believe God just told me that He is giving me my running back even while everything hurts. I think I need to push past the physical limitations and just do it."

'Yay!" she agreed and off we went to finish the run.

My longest run since back surgery clocked in at 7.5 miles that day, and I was ECSTATIC! I hurt everywhere and was drained, but I knew now without a shadow of a doubt that all of this–timing of the new gym being built, meeting Janet and the other friends and training with her for the upcoming race- was orchestrated by God. He gave me my running back, and this time it was different.

Chapter 9

Something Is Not Right

◇◇◇

It's a typical Saturday August morning in South Carolina where the air outside is so thick that it overwhelms me as I open the front door to my two-story brick home. The temperatures are so high that the air conditioning I'm enjoying feels too good to trade for a quick run outside, even on my shaded neighborhood trails. The sun has yet to make its appearance, and I hurry to get dressed so that I can welcome yet another start to a usual summer day. This is my favorite way to usher in God's new mercies while the birds are singing, and the silence is exhilarating while the rest of the world lies asleep.

Like most days, I'm ready to push past my feelings of comfort to experience all the benefits I get from exercising out in nature. My body is saying no, but my brain is saying, "GO!" I'm becoming an expert now in not listening to what symptoms my body is telling me. Chronic illness for the past 25 years has taught me that if I listen and give in, I will never do much of anything, especially relating to exercise. And, since my passion and career lie in the health and fitness field, it's important that I hold myself to a high standard of excellence so that I'm able to lead my people well. Giving up is a choice and not one I'm willing to take.

My son has this Tigger alarm clock that I love because it announces the waking time with Tigger's signature "Hoohoo hoohoo, hoohoo hoohoo, time to bounce!" "Hoohoo hoohoo,

hoohoo hoohoo, time to bounce!" It makes me automatically feel energized and happy and ready to start the day. If I wasn't a morning person, this could serve as an awful annoyance because grumpy morning people aren't too welcoming of jovial early morning talkers. I admit that I'm one of those who gets up ready to roll, and my kids, especially the teenagers, are not impressed. I realize now why I love this alarm clock so much. Think for a minute about the other characters in Winnie the Pooh, especially Eeyore with his large gray donkey body, drooping eyes and black tail, and doom and gloom pessimistic personality. If I didn't know any better, I would guess the creators put that bright pink bow on the end of the tail to give us all a little smile; otherwise, we may join him in the pit of depression. Tigger, on the other hand, is vibrantly colored orange with a terrific tiger personality who sees joy and fun all around him. He has no fear and takes life as it comes, keeping that bounce in his step no matter the circumstance. That's the way I desire to be!

Since God gave me my running back in April, I am making it part of my routine three to four days each week. Physically, it's a challenge, yet I am discovering a deeper drive to continue. It makes no sense to my logical mind. As my back stiffens, my breathing labors, muscles tighten, neuropathy heightens, and other organs scream of disease, I experience this total dependence on Jesus to pull me through. It's like an outer body experience in the best way, not some twilight mystical thing. It's a kingdom atmosphere here on earth, and it's quickly becoming my happy place.

My prayers are bolder than they've ever been as I seek Him for the "impossible." With man, He says it is impossible but with God everything IS possible; "I" "M" possible. I love this so much! *What is my story?* I regularly ask. Holy Spirit is the amazing teacher Who gives us these answers. "I will instruct you and teach you in the way you should go; I will counsel you with my loving eye on you," Psalm 32:8 says. How cool is it that He always has a "loving eye" on us! I remind myself regularly to not merely read the words but also receive and believe them. Words are powerless apart from belief.

Several doors are opening in response to my strong, confident prayers. God says that we can come boldly to the throne of grace to help us in our time of need (Hebrews 4:16). I feel in my heart that I am supposed to do 50 races in the next two years to build some running history of my own. These races will include varying distances as well as some being on trails, some roads, and some multi-sport. This is going to be incredibly taxing, but I believe it's God's will. If it's not, then He will close the door and redirect me. Now that my aerobics director has asked me to lead the Y running group two days a week, I am sensing the need to have some current racing credibility. Although I am an athlete and have been running throughout the years, I haven't done many races to which I can point my students to build their trust. Let's face it. If I'm going to lead a bunch of runners, they will follow my instruction more if I have a stellar track record of being fast and winning races. Plus, suffering from "invisible illness" feels like my words aren't received or believed, especially when I appear to have it all together like I do.

No one will truly believe how horribly awful I feel, and I can't share the personal details of some of what I am going through because it is too personal. My health is bad. My life is full of friction. How am I supposed to make sense of any of this? I can't think about it because it's too much for any one person to handle. My emotions are all over the place, and I want to be stable like Jesus. One minute, I'm peaceful and thanking You for all my wonderful blessings and the next I am engulfed with so much anger and jealousy over what I don't have. I just do NOT feel well. Why can't I just feel sorry for myself and accept all this ill health and quit! It would be so much easier if my lifestyle reflected my struggles. But they are opposites. I wish someone would feel sorry for me just once! This is so lonely and overwhelming. I guess, God, this is how You are teaching me to trust You more. I hate this. But I love You. It's going to get better! It has to.

I am so afraid to commit to any of this because in no way am I well. As a matter of fact, it seems I'm getting progressively worse. And yet, I KNOW that God put this desire in my heart. I don't understand why. All I can do is be obedient to what He says and say "Yes!" And so, I am. Stepping out in faith requires action. Joshua could not lead the Israelites into the Promised Land until he placed his foot into the water. It was then that God rolled it back, unlike with Moses in the parting of the Red Sea. Going deeper with God demands humility and surrender.

As I lace up my favorite hot pink running shoes to take on a new day, an unusual amount of sweat begins pouring off my forehead and onto the floor as if I had already come back from my run. My joints, and most especially my back, are seizing more than normal and with greater intensity. My arms and legs begin to tremor and lock in place, making it nearly impossible to take another step. My elbows are even throbbing and every part of my being from my head to my toes is aching; it feels like pins and needles everywhere with sharp shooting stabbing pain across my torso. The pain is crippling. I've experienced some of these symptoms in the past but not to this degree and not all at once. *I'm scared, God! What is happening to me*, I say aloud. *Please don't let me die. My family needs me.*

As I make my way slowly upstairs with tears streaming down my cheeks and holding on for dear life to the wooden stair railing, I enter my dark bedroom and pass through to the bathroom. The dizziness has gotten so bad that I can barely walk a straight line, and so I take a break and sit down on the side of the tub. My brain feels extra foggy like I can't formulate a thought, and I'm having trouble taking deep breaths from the pain in my chest. Maybe I'm having a heart attack, I think to myself. There is a strange ringing in my ears, and this is a symptom I am not used to. I feel like I have the flu, but it's summer, and it's not flu season. "What is going on?" I repeat aloud. I am becoming accustomed to talking out loud to God because it really helps me process the answers of what I need to do next. There's something powerful about hearing the voice of the person I believe most, myself. These symptoms are more than the ones that I have come to embrace over the past decades as "normal." Something is very wrong!

The house is quiet with Luke still in bed before he prepares for his daily dose of either a run, bike, or swim workout, along with our two slumbering dogs who prefer that I do my exercise first and then come back an hour later to awaken them for theirs. Even they become lazy during summer break when all the running around seems to take a needed pause. All three active kids are also taking advantage of sleeping in with no organized sport practices that require an early morning wake up call.

My fear heightens as now I take my temperature, and I'm running a high fever; for me that's around 102 degrees because my norm is around 97.5. I begin questioning whether I should wake up Luke or wait a bit longer to see if it passes. Because of all the past years of my differing symptoms, it is, for the most part, becoming a topic that he and I don't discuss well together. It's so hard to look like I am OK and doing great because of all the strenuous things I am pushing myself to do when inside my heart is reeling from the truth. But today, there's a lot to see, so I decide to wake him up.

"Luke, Luke!!!" I urgently exclaim as I press on his shoulder.

"What? What's wrong?" he replies.

"Something is wrong! These are not my normal symptoms, and I'm really scared." I answer.

"What do you want me to do?" he says.

"I'm not sure, but something is SERIOUSLY wrong! I literally feel like I am dying!"

Clearly, Luke can tell that I am hurting and quickly gets out of bed. I change my sweat soaked shirt and replace it with a more comfortable t-shirt. As I unhook my sports bra, I notice something moving in my mid back. I immediately grab a small mirror from under my sink and notice a large red area and something wiggling. At closer glance, it seems to be embedded and still alive. I feel like I'm going to pass out. My body is so weak and in so much pain and now my mind is going to the worst unknown places. *Take some deep breaths, I keep saying in my head. It's going to be OK. It's going to be OK.*

"Luke, can you come look at this in my back?" I say calling from the bathroom. "I think it's a tick, and it's still alive!"

He quickly comes to take a closer look and confirms that it is a tick and that it is still alive. All I know to do is try to remove it carefully with tweezers and put it in a zip lock bag to take to the doctor. So, I have Luke remove it and secure it in a plastic bag. I wash the area with soap and water and lie down on my bed for a while to rest while my symptoms begin disappearing within the hour.

"I'll call the doctor on Monday," I tell Luke as he comes to check on me. "I'm feeling better now so I can wait until then."

"OK, if you're sure," he says.

"I am," I reply and quickly fall asleep.

Monday comes after what seems to be weeks of waiting, and I am eager to call the doctor and schedule an appointment. Thankfully, I can get in later that afternoon. My doctor's office is only a five-minute drive from my home, and I arrive ready for answers. I'm back to feeling my normal self again, which is managing the same symptoms I do on a regular basis. In the waiting room, my mind begins racing with thoughts of fear, anxiety, and stress. Quickly, I turn to prayer to quiet my soul.

God, I'm so tired of coming to doctors and not having any real answers to fix my problems. I'm sick, and I need help. What happened to me on Saturday really frightened me, and I don't want to die. I feel like no matter what I do, it's not working the way I want it to, and it's deeply affecting not only me but my marriage and family. I'm really trying to do the right thing which is so hard, and I'm worn out. I'm tired of being sick and tired. This pain is too much to bear. I wish sometimes I could just quit but the hope within me keeps me going for another minute, and the next, and the next; one small step at a time. Please bring me answers today with some solutions that can turn all this around. How am I supposed to do all this running stuff You want me to do when this is going on repeatedly? I know You love me, but it doesn't

*feel like it. Help my feelings catch up. All I know
to do is keep trusting You even when none of this
makes sense, and it doesn't! Please heal me! I can't
take this anymore.*

Feeling a sense of peace now and ready to head back to see the doctor, the nurse calls my name and smiles as we greet one another because we certainly are not strangers. I am here quite a bit these days. She walks me down the hall to the end room as we make small talk about the weather and our families.

"What brings you in today, Erin?" my nurse asks and begins to chart the details I give her about my episode on Saturday.

A few minutes go by, and my doctor enters the room. He is a family friend whom we trust and appreciate having in our medical corner.

"We don't know much about Lyme disease, and I'm not sure if we have it in this area of South Carolina but let's test you just in case since you appear to have had many of the symptoms," he says. "Wait here and someone will be in to take your blood."

Lyme disease is a bacterial infection from the bite of an infected tick. Also, now it is believed that mosquitos and other rodents can carry the bacteria. If caught early, it responds effectively to antibiotic treatment. If left untreated early, it can spread to the joints, heart, and nervous system.

"OK," I hesitantly reply. After being seen in so many different doctor's offices over the years, I'm tired of being disappointed, yet again, with no real solid answers. I know it sounds a bit crazy, but I'm hoping it will show positive. I don't really like the phrase, "ignorance is bliss" because I think it's another excuse for people not to take responsibility for their own health and life. I want to know! Knowledge, to me, is so important because then at least I can work to be part of the solution. We are told to steward this "temple" well, the Bible says, and I hold that value high.

The 15 minutes turn into at least 30 and, by now, I am growing antsy. I finally hear a knock on the door, and my doctor returns to tell me that the results from the Western Blot and Elisa tests are negative. These are the two tests commonly used by Western medical doctors to test for Lyme disease while the percentage of accuracy is only around 40%. He decides to prescribe me Doxycycline, a broad-spectrum antibiotic, for 10 days to cover me in case I have the disease. I want to cry or maybe scream. I don't know any more how much of this I can take. I want to feel good. And so, I leave with a big pit in my stomach wondering how I'm going to take another antibiotic after 20 years of taking upwards of 10 per year for chronic sinus infections that are wreaking havoc on my gut. I feel like I'm back to square one.

I pick up my prescription at the local pharmacy and immediately take it when I arrive home. I'm so scared to take another round of powerful antibiotics because I'm not sure I can handle anymore fungal related infections on top of my normal load. Every week for too many years to count, I am dealing with unwanted side effects from these medicines. I absolutely hate taking them, but my body hasn't seemed to be able to function without them. I know they are destroying my gut, but I don't know what else to do. I continue seeking God for answers and following through the doors He opens, so I'm doing now what I know to do: take the antibiotic with some probiotics and trust all will be well. Probiotics are live microorganisms that are intended to have health benefits when consumed or applied to the body. They fill the gut with good bacteria while antibiotics take out the good and bad because they can't discriminate. They kill the infection but also wipe out the beneficial.

My fitness classes and running continue, but after several days on this medicine, I am experiencing severe side effects and end up calling my doctor for advice. The nerve pain throughout my body is increasing again. My head is pounding, joints are aching, and my gut is reeling with pain. The nurse advises me to discontinue taking the medicine, and without me knowing much about what's driving these flares, I heed her advice and immediately stop. I turn it over to God and beg for this to be taken from me. He's my only hope.

Chapter 10

A Warrior Heart

Fifty races in two years. That is what I heard God say to me, and I am determined to see it come to pass. I have my reasons and try explaining it to my husband but feel like I really am not taken seriously. I am mad at him for not believing I can do this but don't blame him either. After all, I really don't believe in my ability either, yet I am the one doing all the training and racing. How can you really be "that sick" and still do what you are doing? On paper, it isn't possible, yet I do it. Being overwhelmed sets the stage for God to work. It's our job to lay it down and agree with Him.

God told Moses in Exodus 4 to throw his staff to the ground. Moses had a fear of man and didn't feel equipped to carry out the work God was calling him to. The staff became a snake as it hit the ground. As God told him to pick it up again, it returned to a staff in his hand. This is a beautiful image and symbol of surrender. We must remove the things of the flesh that interfere with God's willingness to work. It's a painful process. I love the wording of "throwing down" because that implies force. It hurts to release a lot of our fleshly sinful nature and desire. For me it's things like fear, pride, worry, anger, jealousy, unbelief, and rejection. And it won't be a one time "throw down" but, instead, a continual process of letting go and letting God.

I have 50 opportunities to train and anticipate the challenge like nothing before in my life. This two-year period of racing is changing me and becoming not only a test of my will to finish the impossible feat but also the vehicle taking me into deeper spiritual places. People are built to do hard things. We can choose to succumb to our circumstances and be ruled by feelings or step into the atmosphere of supernatural strength powered by the Holy Spirit. I want to be in the game and not a spectator in my own life. I yearn for these moments of feeling God's perfect power in my weakness. Being able to run strong is my spiritual high that I need to stay the course while my miracles are still in motion. I experience many small ones along the way but not the big breakthroughs that I am trusting and believing God for. Some things God takes care of by His own working, but most require us to perform an action. Sometimes that action leads to work, which can take a long time. The Bible says that we are "co-laborers with Christ" which means we have a part to do. This is my part, though I don't have the "why" answered but only the "what." He doesn't promise to tell us everything. I have my prepared "YES" in my spirit and press on to see where He will take me. The more difficult the challenge the more fruitful the reward.

I don't know where this is taking me God, but I know Your hand is in it. People are judging and doubting me, though I know this is what You called me into. There is no way my physical body in this condition can do all of this, and I know it's going to wear me out, and I will pay for it later. That's OK because I'd rather deal with that repercussion of worsening health than disobeying You. I am a soldier in the army of God, and this is calling me into a confidence and boldness of strength that excites and frightens me all at the same time. I don't want the quarreling with my husband, but I can handle it if You are my rock. I'm overwhelmed and scared but also super exhilarated. I'm ready to run my race and experience You working. This is the place that I can see and hear You the most. I CAN do all things through Christ who gives me strength (Philippians 4:13). Help open eyes of others to see You working through me and let me be a testimony of Your goodness, willingness, and faithfulness.

The races I completed came in various distances and venues. I completed all the trail races from a 5k distance through the 21k distance. The "k" stands for kilometers, so the distances ranged from 3.1 miles to a half marathon, 13.1 miles. I ran regular road races from a 5k to half marathon and completed a duathlon series ranging from a sprint to an Olympic distance. A duathlon is a multisport and involves doing a run at the beginning followed by a bike leg and finishing with another run leg. The distances ranged from a mile on the initial run to a 10k which is 6.2 miles. The bike portion was anywhere from 13 miles to 28 miles. I won the YMCA duathlon series for female competitors. In the other races, I also proved successful in terms of placement finishing. Most every race I competed in, I either won my age group (which was age 40-44) or the master's overall division. There were several trail races where I finished top three female overall, and the only races I didn't place were in the Cooper River Bridge runs that had 40,000+ runners. Even in that one, I finished in the top 10% of females my age. I won prizes including new trail running shoes, North Face pullovers, watches, backpacks, gift cards, smart wool socks and hats, and even beer for a year! Since I'm not a beer drinker, I gave that prize away to a willing young gentleman who acted as if I had given him a new car! I won prizes that were super nice, and I was literally blown away and deeply humbled every time I heard my name called and walked before the crowd to receive my prize. I say all this not to boast in my abilities, but to point to the power of Christ who strengthens and rests on me. These results are applaudable by healthy individuals training a lot and yet I am not that person. Learning to train shorter and smarter is my new way of living.

I stand in AWE every time at how God works through me, and I make sure to point to Him to receive all the glory and honor. I simply say 'YES" and step into the atmosphere of supernatural living, and it quickly becomes my happy place. I share these stories of victories with my running friends, runners I coach through my YMCA Team FAST running team, social media sites, fitness classes I lead, friends/neighbors/family members, and any places God showers me with influence. I open myself up to living out loud and direct anyone who listens to the goodness of God. It is both a gift and a curse. Racing is saving my life by supplying a reason to keep fighting through the pain and depleting the resources I have all at the same time. But God! He never fails to show up. When there is no way, He makes a way!

The best part of these two years has been the incredible moments I have had with my kids. My middle child travels to many races with me and competes as well. Some races we travel three hours one way and make fun day trips out of or an overnight hotel adventure. I know that God ordains this time for different reasons, and this is a big one!

As a mom, I regularly carve out one-on-one time with all three kids. I believe it is important to spend individual moments together investing in them. They are my motivation to press on and seek to live a life of excellence. And they are super fun humans with whom I love spending time. Don't get me wrong, we have our share of normal dysfunctional family dynamics, but, overall, they are the reason I get up each morning and am determined to go the distance. They push me to be my best without probably ever knowing the impact they have. My problems fade with them around. I need a distraction from my thoughts. Being a parent will do that. Our family fun centers around outdoors, sports, and racing. They set my competitive drive into lesser gear when they take center stage.

One of my favorite races as I began this journey took place in Fort Mill, SC, a short two-hour drive from my home. It was a sprint distance duathlon and my second one to participate in. It was a mile run followed by a 16-mile bike ending with a 3.1-mile run.

The week began in typical Erin fashion, being on a strong antibiotic and prednisone for yet another sinus infection and severe allergy symptoms. This was my fourth one in six months. I did the minimal amount of training to get by and still be competitive. It was a constant balance of not doing too much and not doing enough. By mid-week, my symptoms worsened, and the doctor changed my antibiotic. I had the hotel already booked and needed to leave that Friday for Saturday's race. I taught a couple of bike and fitness classes that week as per usual and only went outside whenever needed and stayed off all trails to not aggravate symptoms. I watched my diet closely and avoided unnecessary sugars, dairy, caffeine, and anything else that triggered more unwanted symptoms.

My oldest son was 15 years old at the time, and he decided that he would do the triathlon. That was a swim, bike, and run. Both events were together, and he was a good swimmer. All week

I mentioned to him about training and being young and carefree, his response was, "I got it!"

"The course has a lot of big rolling hills," I said. "You need to get on your bike and at least put in a few training days."

"I'm good," he confidently responded.

"OK, then, but I don't think you're going to be prepared but that's on you," I answered.

Friday afternoon arrived and with all three kids I headed for Fort Mill. Luke stayed behind to watch dogs and do his usual Saturday morning training with his running group. I was still feeling sick, but we had paid money for both races, and I wanted to go. My allergies made it very challenging to do much of anything. I was perpetually dizzy to the point that driving proved difficult and many times I could only go short distances because of fear of not getting back. Foods I ate caused flare ups, and I never knew when it may worsen. Water even bothered me, and I was unable to do regular electrolyte drinks like Gatorade because my gut situation triggered infections, flare ups and pain. It took a lot of management merely to do an event like this one, but I felt God was in it, and it was meant to be.

Upon arriving at the hotel, the kids and I unloaded the two bikes and brought in all our suitcases and gear, and for triathlons or multisport events then you know that it's a lot. My daughter volunteered to come along to look after her nine-year-old brother while my oldest son and I raced. I was so excited to have all three kids here with me because this, to me, was what being a mom was all about—doing life alongside my family. We ventured out to the nearest Olive Garden restaurant for our pre-race pasta meal. I received a text message from my husband stating that I forgot my main suitcase at home on our bed. It contained all my racing clothes. Quickly, I called back.

"What am I going to do? I need all of this, or I can't race," I said as the tears began to form.

"I know. That's why I texted you. I can't help because I am heading to dinner with customers in 20 minutes. I guess you won't be able to do the race," he said.

I sat quietly for a moment to gather my thoughts because not racing was not an option. I couldn't drive the two hours back to Greenville and then two hours back to Fort Mill because it already was after 6:00 pm, and the race tomorrow started at 7:30 am. I began to cry at the table in the middle of the restaurant. We ordered food already, but now we needed to leave. I didn't feel well to start with and now I had this to deal with.

> *I can't do this, God. I don't understand why You lead*
> *me to do these things and then stuff like this happens.*
> *It's WAY too much for me. Feeling as sick and broken*
> *down as I do is hard enough and now this happens! I*
> *can't catch a break. I want to quit, but I can't. Why*
> *can't I just give in and quit?*

A thought popped in my head to call my parents and see if they could help.

"Mom, I left my suitcase at home, and I need it. Would you and Dad be able to drive halfway and meet me with it? I barely feel well enough to do this race tomorrow and now I have this to contend with. I don't even know if I can drive another couple of hours with the kids too, but I don't have a choice. They have to ride along because I'm not comfortable leaving them at the hotel alone. We just ordered our food and so I need to wait for it, but the kids can take it to go and eat in the car. I need my stuff in that suitcase so I can race," I said.

Mom responded, "We can meet you at the gas station in Black Mountain in an hour and a half. We will go get your suitcase now and text you the exit number and other details. It's going to be OK. We will see you soon. Drive carefully, and I love you."

While the waitress proceeded to box up our food for the road trip at hand, I wanted to throw the biggest tantrum and scream, "I QUIT!!!!!!!" Loading up the kids and the food, we drove to make the hand off without time to socialize with Mom and Dad.

"Thank you SO much!" I said to Mom and Dad as I received my things. "I literally do not know what I would do without you both! I owe you big time."

"We are happy to help and so glad it wasn't tomorrow morning when you learned you didn't have your stuff!" they replied.

"Oh gosh, me too," I responded. And with that, we gave hugs, and I headed back north for our hotel.

I was exhausted. I was tired from a week of being a wife, mom, homemaker, fitness instructor, and athlete, and being sick and on medication. Now it was after 9:00 pm, and I had wanted to be asleep by now for our 5:00 am wake up call. Was I even going to be able to do this race tomorrow, I thought? I felt like I had no choice. I had made it this far, and the show must go on. And it did.

The alarm came quickly as I hadn't slept much after all the shenanigans the night before. We got to the race site with plenty of time to park, check in, get body marked, and set up our stuff. I gave some money to my daughter to get some breakfast while they waited for us to finish. They could watch us start and be at the finish area to see us come in about an hour and a half later.

I took my place at the Start Line after wishing my son a good race. I was nervous for him because he didn't really train. He was a good athlete by default and was in shape from summer swimming and cross country but not so much on the bike. His start took place in the pool with a swim and mine with a mile run so we parted ways and said, "I'll see you at the Finish Line!"

God, I am a nervous wreck. My back is bad, and I don't feel well and there's no way I can do this. But I'm here, and I need You to show up. Thank You for getting me to this point. I want to bring You glory in this so please help me and my son. Keep us safe and let us run with endurance the race marked out for us!

The gun sounded, and about 50 other runners took off with me. The duathlon pack was always smaller as most participants do the triathlon. I finished the first mile at a 7:42 pace, and I was happy with that. I gutted the entire mile out and didn't care about having too much in the tank for the last run leg. I felt weak and dizzy, not my best, but also not my worst. I set a goal to do the first run leg under eight minutes and have a strong bike leg. I taught cycle classes but didn't do much riding outside. I was strong on the bike, though, and desired to have a fast split.

I transitioned from my running shoes to my bike shoes which clipped into the pedals, buckled my helmet, and jogged alongside the bike to the end of the transition area. There, I quickly mounted my bike and took off. I loved my bike. It was a red colored, very lightweight road bike with carbon build and narrow tires. It's a bike meant to race but not top of the line, by any means. But it worked for me. I named her Faith, and "Big Red" was her racing nickname. I taped a special reminder on the bar in front of my seat that read: Perseverance…I can do all things through Christ who gives me strength. I wanted it always placed in front of me as my reminder to not give up! Our bike shop friends had fitted it to me and positioned my handlebars as far upward and forward as possible to help ease my back pain. Since biking strains the back, and that strain leads down the legs and into the feet, it can challenge that last run leg in a big way.

The hills were rolling and big! I remember climbing this one around mile 12 and thinking there's no way that my son is going to do this well. This was a hard course for those of us who had trained and without training, it was very difficult. *Help him, God! This is hard, and we both need Your help.*

I rounded the final turn approaching the transition area and the volunteer yelled to me, "You are the first female! Keep it up. You're killing it!" I smiled with exhaustion yet exhilaration. I can't believe this is happening. I came in with the 17th overall fastest bike split that day out of 187 total finishers, male and female. I was thrilled with that time and meeting that goal.

Getting off the bike was demanding. My legs were exhausted from that hard ride, and I gave it everything I had. The first mile was the hardest because my back stiffened so much accompanied by the nerve pain everywhere, but I pushed through. The course wove through a nearby neighborhood, and I remember taking 10-15 second intermittent walk breaks because the dizziness took hold so powerfully. It didn't scare me because I was used to this, but it did cause me to walk at times. I was on my eight-minute mile pace, but I felt like I was going to black out. By now the sun was out, and it was hot and humid. I was exhausted and depleted but determined to finish strong and keep my first-place female position. *I wonder how the boy is doing. I hope he's OK. I may have to go find him when I'm done. This is a tough race.* And I pressed on.

Coming into the last turn, I heard the cheers and cowbells from spectators and spotted my other two kids down the hill at the blue and white Finish Line blow up arch.

They clapped and cheered, "Go Mom! Finish strong!" I could see the excitement and pride in their faces. I opened my running stride as I neared that final 20 meters, and a smile appeared on my face. It was finally over, and I made it. I did it.

"Mom! Mom!" I heard yelling loudly from behind. As I looked over my shoulder there was my son in an all-out sprint chasing me down. I felt relief and elation all at once. I could see the grimace in his face to catch me and thought, had he been behind me the entire time?

With linked hands, we crossed the Finish Line together, and a smile so big filled my heart that I believed I may burst open at any moment.

"Where did you come from?" I breathlessly asked.

"I have been chasing you down since I saw you on the bike course on the turnaround. You were way ahead of me," he said.

"Wow! You must have really had a great bike split!" I responded.

"I did, but why didn't you make me train?" he laughed.

I sat on the curb taking turns posing for post-race pictures and sharing race details. The happiness and joy I felt couldn't be put into words. Yes, the first-place finishes by both of us were great, but it wasn't about that. I was here with three people I loved most in the world. It was fun and challenging, and I loved a challenge.

We four shared hugs and congratulations and enjoyed the fruits of our labor. God did it again. His perfect power made known in my weakness. How will anyone believe me that I was that sick and still did this well? God will have to work that part out. I showed up and did mine. I can't make people see what they need to see or hear what they can't hear. Only God can cause hearts to believe. But it doesn't make it any easier being misunderstood.

That image of my son coming around that final turn in a full on, outstretched sprint impacted my life in a profound way. It isn't a race to beat me but a moment in time that expresses the heart of a champion. I see David running into battle to come up against Goliath, no hesitation, and no fear. I want that warrior heart to run down any "giants" that God places in my path.

God knew the outcome before we said "YES" and to think I would have missed it all over a forgotten suitcase and week of being sick. These are the moments I long for. The moments of impossible turned possible with each step. Athletes often complain of being out of breath and incurring other physical ailments like fast heart rate, but to me it signals life. This reminds me that I'm alive. Though I hate muscles cramping and pain moving throughout my body, at least I can feel it all, and I have a body! Attitude is everything.

The favor of God showed up in the 11th hour with a storybook ending and one that only He can write. He is the author of our life, and we solely supply the pictures on the page. This page makes my heart smile BIG!

Chapter 11

Put On Your Big Girl Pants

Ring, ring, ring. Ring, ring, ring.

"Hello," Luke answers, finally picking up the phone on the last ring before going to voicemail.

"I, I, I am not going to make it, Luke," I stutter, barely able to get out the words between each uncontrollable sob. It's all I can do to talk, but I need to share my heart right now because it's breaking.

"What are you talking about?" he says. "Can we talk about this later because I'm at lunch with a customer? Can I call you back when we're done?"

"No!" I emphatically respond. "I'll be quick. I'm going to die! I mean it. My body can't do this anymore. I'm only 42 years old but I'm either going to die by age 50 if I can even make it that long or have a rebirth if God turns things around. Of course, that's what I'm praying for and holding out for, but I need a breakthrough now. Like, in the real world here, I need answers. I can't do this anymore. I can't take it. It's too much for any one person to bear. I am dying, Luke."

"Erin, why do you say that? You're not going to die. I have to go, but I'll call you back in a little while. I love you," he answers and hangs up.

I am driving back from a consultation I had with a different nutritionist who was recommended by a friend. The nutritionist lives in Charlotte, North Carolina, about an hour and a half one-way drive. The appointment has me very anxious, depressed, and stressed out. I am crying alone in the car once again and talking to Jesus. This seems to be a regular pattern now. Anytime I am alone away from kids, I break out into tears over the situation in my life. I feel isolated and tired of being at odds over my health with my husband. This appointment, again, wasn't covered by insurance, and I feel like a constant drain on our finances. I feel like a burden, though I didn't ask for any of this and am still trying to find healthy solutions to getting well. I am so tired of explaining why I need more money. It feels like I am drifting on an island all alone. Of course, God is there with me, but I wish I had my husband's emotional support too. I assume he talks to God about me and our struggles, but I don't really know because I'm the only one who regularly shares verbally what's on my heart. I am very frustrated.

This nutritionist, Mary, seems to know her stuff, and I like her OK. She isn't warm and fuzzy but that's all right if she can help me. We spend two hours going over my two-week food journal with her making suggestions on what I need for better health results. To be honest, it's all so overwhelming. I don't even know where to start. It seems like I already have given up so many foods, yet I'm still having problems. I believe that nutrition is one area we can control in our lives and can cause a positive or negative difference in wellness based on our choices. I had thought I was eating well until she and I met. I am starting over again, having to give up everything that tastes good because my menu keeps narrowing. She performed some testing, and the results will take a month to come back, so she said she would call me as to how to proceed. It's Halloween afternoon, and all I can think about now is getting home and getting candy ready for trick or treaters and getting my youngest picked up from school then dressed in his pirate's costume.

> *God, I don't know how to handle all of this. I feel like I'm dying, and I don't know how to make it stop. Please give me some answers from these tests I had done today. I need answers and solutions. I need You to fix this.*

Weeks pass, and I am preparing for my last half marathon of the year in two weeks when my phone rings.

"Hi Erin, this is Mary from Integrative Health. You came to see me four weeks ago, and I have your results to go over if you have time now or we can schedule a phone appointment," she says.

"Hi Mary," I say. "Now is actually a good time because I am at my computer and kids are all in school."

"OK, great," she answers and proceeds to send me the results via email so we can look them over together.

There are multiple pages, around 20, and, one by one, we go through the results together. It shows a lot of red flags towards foods that I can't tolerate but many of these are ones I already knew from past years of food and allergy testing. This is not anything new to me until she gets to one area that is highlighted.

"You have a high gluten intolerance, and my advice is that you go gluten free immediately! I think if you do this one thing alone, it will give you a lot of relief. It may not solve all your problems, but I believe it will make a big impact on your overall health and well-being. Dairy is also a problem for most people and you too, I believe. It wouldn't hurt giving that up too, especially with all your allergy and sinus problems."

Taking it all in, I'm dazed with all kinds of crazy scenarios running through my brain. How am I going to do this race? What am I going to eat? How am I going to cook now for my family? I have two teenagers and an elementary aged child. What are they going to eat? Am I going to be able to enjoy anything again in my life? How will I travel and what will I eat? Now, what do I have to give up?

Quickly calming these thoughts so that I can reply, "OK, I feel gob smacked but also happy to have some answers. Thank you."

"I also think it would be wise to seek out a good gastroenterologist and have him/her test you for celiac disease. If you have celiac, it's imperative that you strictly adjust your diet, and they can go over all of that with you," Mary says.

Gluten is a protein found in the wheat plant and some other grains. It is naturally occurring, but it can be extracted, concentrated, and added to food and other products to add protein, texture, and flavor. It also works as a binding agent to hold processed foods together and give them shape. It's common in foods such as bread, pasta, pizza, and cereal. Gluten provides no essential nutrients. People with celiac disease have an immune reaction that is triggered by eating gluten. They develop inflammation and damage in their intestinal tracts and other parts of the body when they eat foods containing gluten.

Ending our conversation allows me to process some of what I just heard. I spin my chair around facing my file cabinet and laying my head down between my sweaty clammy hands, I begin to sob. It hurts to think right now so I allow myself to cry, and cry I do. I am so glad that no one is home because I need some time to be alone, cry, think, and pray. The dogs are looking on as if to say, what is wrong with her? Ten minutes pass, and it's time to pull myself together and plan. As always, I seek God first for wisdom and allow answers to come. Maybe this is the answer I have been praying for since I was a kid and cannot remember a time that my stomach seemed settled. Maybe this is the silver bullet, the missing puzzle piece. Maybe this is God answering my prayers…. finally!

I flip through my nearby Bible, which I'm not in a good habit of reading or studying apart from every-once-in-awhile, organized Bible studies, or in a Sunday morning church service. I know I need to make more time to get in the Word, but I am so busy with life that I can't find the time. Plus, I don't seem to be able to understand all the scriptures like I want to and get discouraged and quit. I like verses and parables that point to needs or celebrations in my life, and so I sort of pick and choose those. I desire to read the Bible and study it more, but I find it rather boring and have guilt for feeling that way. I do read my daily devotionals most days and look up verses that I like. I am praying on a regular basis for God to give me a heart that gets excited to go to church and read my Bible. I love God, but I want to feel an outpouring in this tangible way. So far, I don't have that feeling yet, but I continue asking, seeking, and knocking.

First, we perform the right action and then feelings catch up later. It may take some time, so we can't give up in the process of a true heart transformation. Behavioral change is fleeting while transformation of the heart is a renewal that no longer conforms to the ways of the world. It pleases God. One is based on the flesh while the other the spirit man. One of my favorite stories in the Bible is in John chapter 5. It's about the healing of the invalid at the pool of Bethesda. I love this story because it shows what a victim mentality looks like, the opposite of what I desire to have. We all have a choice in handling our circumstances. Bad circumstances affect us all, and we can choose to be a victim or a victor. God calls us to come up higher.

In this story, there were a great number of disabled people waiting around this pool during times when Jesus went to Jerusalem for a feast of the Jews. These people included the paralyzed, blind, and the lame. The pool was believed to have healing powers. There was one invalid who had been there for 38 years. Jesus asked him if he wanted to get better and his reply was, "Sir, I have no one to help me into the pool when the water is stirred. While I am trying to get in, someone else goes down ahead of me." He was waiting for others to come do the work for him.

Jesus commands him to "Get up! Pick up your mat and walk!" and instantly the invalid is cured. It's our personal responsibility to keep getting up no matter how many times we are knocked down by the circumstances of life. Action is required along with releasing faith! God has one direction and that is forward.

I give myself a little pep talk, and the crying ceases. I do it often, and it helps. I call my gastroenterologist who looks at all things gut related and schedule an appointment. They can't get me in for several months, and I need to be eating gluten-containing foods a couple weeks out from my office visit to get accurate test results. In the meantime, I heed the advice of my nutritionist and begin the research in going gluten free. Thankfully, it's a lot easier eating this way in 2011 than it was back in the 1980s when these gut issues first manifested. I decide to eat healthily all the way around, focusing on whole, plant-based foods. I don't want to trade gluten containing foods for gluten free boxed foods. I want to limit eating out of a bag or box altogether and stick with eating real foods. I start with snacks because there will be times that I can't prepare a fresh healthy meal and will need to have something on standby to pull me through. For instance, a good healthy gluten free energy bar I can keep in my purse for emergency situations like being on a field trip with one of the kids or at a party or friend's house where gluten free options aren't readily available. Gathering my snack options list together and going to the local health food store is my first order of business. I can do this. I can go little by little or pull the band aid right off and begin a gluten free lifestyle. It's going to be difficult, but I can do it if God is on my side. I hate this, but it is what it is. I am ready to be well, so I will do whatever it takes, even if it means giving up my favorite Greek yogurts and milk chocolate treats. Surely, there is a decadent dark chocolate alternative that I will love. Rip goes the band aid!

The appointment with the specialist turns into multiple visits including extensive testing for celiac disease. Gratefully, all my tests come back negative for carrying the celiac gene, but I am diagnosed with non-celiac gluten intolerance. Basically, that means I need to be off any gluten containing foods–mostly everything aside from plain meats, fruits, and vegetables. For a period after having these endoscopic procedures, I am once again doubling over in pain. The doctors try giving me different medicines to calm it down, but it eventually subsides on its own.

I continue leading my YMCA running group, including taking them to their first organized race as well as checking off more races in my "50 races in two years" quest. My back bothers me so much on my road bike, and I am so upset with not being able to ride it as much as I would like that I spent my Christmas money on a cheap bike from Costco that sits up higher and has a comfy seat. When life throws lemons, make lemonade. There is always another option or direction to go if we're willing to keep asking, keep seeking, and keep knocking. God opens doors that no man can close and closes doors that no man can open. Life is fluid. Quitting is an option but so is enduring. I feel like an old woman buying a commuter bike, but I would rather do something than nothing at all. And, at this point, I am quickly running out of movement options. Swimming provokes too much nerve pain, and walking aggravates my back problems worse than running. Since I can't run all the time, that leaves me limited choices. Where there is a will, there is a way.

I learn everything I can about healthier cooking and eating. I feel like a student of nutrition therapy. I am researching voraciously on the internet and taking all kinds of notes as well as watching television shows like *Dr. Oz* where he has so many good nutritionists and holistic doctors who are teaching me healthier habits. One thing keeps leading to another and another, and I'm learning so much. It's yet another big mountain to overcome, and I'm not experiencing much symptom relief yet, but I believe it will take time and it will happen. What's the saying, Rome wasn't built in a day? I can't expect decades of eating incorrectly to magically turn around in a few months. However, I am noticing a lot less stomach bloat and an overall feeling of being healthier, thus I am eager to keep learning and getting better. It's not easy making double meals at home, but for now, it's easiest for me this way. If I make spaghetti, for example, I give my family the regular meat sauce and pasta noodles while I simply eat the sauce with gluten free pasta. I hope to transition them over soon as well, but kids are picky so I'm breaking them in slowly. I'm cooking most meals with meat and several vegetables. I can't eat sauces, so everything is bland, but that's fine by me. The youngest is having the hardest time, especially since his days are determined by the daily menu. He asked me recently, "Can we have potatoes from Idaho like everyone else?" when I showed him the purple medley mix of new potatoes that I was preparing. Getting healthier is another growing pain for all of us. At the end of the day, though, I still wish God would fix this all Himself instead of my having to do so much work. It's one thing to cook like this if you feel well and yet another if you feel lousy. I need a chef!

Chapter 12

Yes, You Can!

◇◇◇◇◇◇◇◇◇◇◇◇◇◇◇◇◇◇◇◇◇

July is officially here, and summer in the South continues with its high humidity and heat. Janet and I are determined to get our run in before it heats up to unbearable conditions. We especially like to meet at a church that backs up to our city's paved trail system. There are a lot of large trees along the seven-mile route we plan to run today, so we can get some much-needed shade. As always, we run and talk, sharing everything that's been going on in our lives during that week, including stories of our families and what they are up to. Today is no different except that I am really struggling to take each step since I am dealing with so many flare-ups. Janet knows about the doctor I began seeing back in February and how he is ordained by God, I believe. He came into my life through a friend, and the timing was certainly His. I don't mind the three-hour drive down to Charleston either because my in-laws live near there at the beach, so I'm able to make a little trip out of it and stay with them. I love them both dearly, and we all have a great time together. I have been down that way for appointments now probably three or four times, and with all the testing I recently completed, it's a mere couple of weeks before my results are finally back. This is going to possibly be a game changer in my life, and I am filled with eager anticipation.

Janet is telling me all about a Run For God program that she is beginning in the fall. It's a program started by a man who is from the Georgia area. He started this program to encourage others to deepen their love of running while strengthening their relationship with the Lord. He himself is a runner and knows the importance of honoring God through our hobbies. The program is a 12-week training program that parallels faith and endurance. Since the Bible is filled with analogies and metaphors of our life being like a running race, my interest is piqued.

"I am so excited about all the people that have already signed up! I am going to have another lady helping me, and we are going to have it at our church. Most of the training runs will probably take place somewhere else because we don't really have the space, but I'm working all of that out now," Janet says happily. "We are starting the middle of September with our destination race in December before Christmas. I can't wait."

"That sounds awesome! I wish I would've thought of that myself since I kind of feel like I have been doing that program without even knowing it existed," I laugh. "Too bad I didn't think of it first because that's a program I love and can totally relate to!"

The running and small talk continue as we near this hilly section that causes our heart rates to soar and breathing labor. The lawn crew is out mowing the grass, and our eyes begin to feel the pollen in the air. My dizziness intensifies forcing me to stop for a brief walking break.

Janet looks at me instantly and proclaims, "WAIT a MINUTE!!!! WHY aren't YOU doing a Run For God program at your church? You ARE the poster child for Run For God!"

Pausing for a moment, I feel my spirit fill with confirmation.

"Yes, now that you say it out loud, I totally agree with you!" I comment. "The problem is that I am the most broken that I have ever been and how the heck am I going to lead not only the speaking/study portion but the running part? It's all I can do right now as you can tell, to walk, let alone run. Your church is small too and mine is huge. I would probably have like a hundred people or something. Plus, I am still waiting for my results to come back, so I don't even know what direction God is leading me in. I have SO many balls up in the air, it blows me away, so I can't think about it."

"Well, I think you should do it!" she exclaims. "It's not like you don't know what to do and look at what you've been doing already leading all your other running groups and people. You can do it!"

Thinking intently and feeling Holy Spirit convicting me with a slight nudge towards the "YES" decision, I say to Janet,

"OK. I'll pray about it."

What in the world am I thinking? I can't take on this huge project right now when I don't even know what's going to be happening to me in the next few weeks. This is crazy, yet I so desperately want to do this. I feel like it's meant to be. Could God really be in this? I am going to need to spend some time seeking the Lord about it and go from there.

Sitting in church that following Sunday, our pastor begins his sermon and I, per usual, am listening closely and taking notes. I don't remember the main title of this sermon, but I do remember what happened when he said something to the effect of God calling us to seasons in our life when nothing seems to make sense. My ears perk up slightly and then his words go mute. It is as if I hear God in an audible voice on both sides of me saying, *you need to bring Run For God to this church.*

As many of us do, I first doubt whether this is even God. How in the world can I take this on now when my life is literally hanging in the balance regarding these test results? And my body and soul are the worst they've ever been, and God is saying He is calling ME to lead a running ministry! Ha! I cannot be hearing this right. Or am I? God called Moses when he felt inept and couldn't speak well. He chose Mary to carry His Son when she was a poor, unwed teenager. And Paul was one of the greatest apostles, yet he first persecuted the Christians. The Bible is full of ordinary people called to do impossible things.

A week goes by and during that time God continues to give me sign after sign through music lyrics, time in the Word, prayer, devotionals, billboards, television shows, other people–you name it -it was like He was not going to let me drop this. I couldn't get it out of my head, and my spirit sang with excitement at the possibility. Is this where God has been leading me? Could all the love I've been feeling in my heart and soul for running be for this moment? I didn't know the exact reasons, but I did know that if I said "No" then I would be disobeying God, and I couldn't bear that thought.

I call my recreation director friend at church, and we meet to discuss my proposal. As we begin talking, I feel complete peace. I have no idea where any of this is going to lead, but I do know one thing and that is all I need—THIS is God's plan for me at this time in this church, and so I begin with that.

"John, thanks so much for meeting me. And, how cool is it that God orchestrated our meeting up again after all these years? To think we played travel soccer together as teenagers back in Ohio and now you are pastoring at the church that my family and I are members of! WOW! It totally blows my mind!" I say.

"I know, right? It's so crazy but so cool," he says. "So, what great things do you have to share with me today? I can't wait to hear about this program that you briefly mentioned to me via email."

"It's called Run For God, and my running friend told me about it during our run recently. She is leading one at her church and encouraged me to lead one at mine. I prayed about it because the timing could not be worse and yet I feel SO deeply in my soul that God is leading me to spearhead this here," I answer.

I proceed to share the details about the strong conviction I had during Sunday's service especially when this scripture came to mind—"I tell you the truth, when you were younger you dressed yourself and went where you wanted; but when you are old you will stretch out your hands, and someone else will dress you and lead you where you do not want to go" (John 21:18).

"God told me I needed to do this, so here I am! I have no details whatsoever on how this will look and to be honest, I don't even know if I will be here for the launch. I'm in limbo, if you will, waiting for important test results to come back and that could change the course of everything," I respond.

Pausing briefly to take it all in, John smiles and says, "You won't believe this. Well, with your faith you probably will. The three pastors and I recently met to discuss dropping our current running program because it didn't have any kind of structured faith component like what you are mentioning. We literally canceled it yesterday! So, this is definitely a move of God, and I'm going to take it to them and get back with you about definite plans. I love the idea, and I can't wait to see where God leads!"

"Me too!" I say, "especially since I am in the worst shape of my life. This should be good."

Saying our so longs, I leave the church building with a peace so serene it envelops my soul. It's like a war going on within me between my body and spirit. The facts from the truth. I don't even know what or how I am going to make it another hour and yet I now have this responsibility of leading a running ministry on the table. I am overwhelmed, terrified, excited, and hopeful all at once.

John calls me a few days later stating, "We are a go!"

Now, I am really terrified.

Days fill with all sorts of emotion and, at times, an avalanche so great that all I can do is take it to God and leave it with Him. When God calls us to an assignment, He will not desert us. There's a plan. There is peace. There is provision. My family and friends question what I am doing, but I can't let that sway me or take me off course. "Trust in the Lord with all your heart and lean not on your own understanding in all your ways, acknowledge him and he will direct your path" (Proverbs 3:5-6). I keep reciting that life verse aloud, and my soul strengthens each time I do. What good is scripture if we merely consider it words in a book. No, we need to put our feet to it, and I am literally doing that now. I learned not to live my life anymore based on the approval of others or public opinion. That means my closest loved ones too. And that is hard. My flesh hates this, that's for sure!

As I share my story with others, I am open to criticism and questioning. God doesn't always have certain hearts prepared just yet to receive the testimony I am displaying before them. But He will bring forth those who need to hear and see it by positioning them to receive. That's His job to do and not mine. It took me a while to get here with thicker skin, and most times it still hurts to feel that rejection, but it's getting easier the more I practice. Life experience increases trust in God. It's a process. It takes time. There are some things we must go through to grow through. I'm learning it's not a personal rejection because then it's about me and that's pride. It's about Him! The Holy Spirit is the enforcer. Jesus himself was mocked. In Mark chapter 3, He was said to be out of His mind and possessed by Beelzebub! That came on the heels of healing many. We must decide whether to be led by fear of man or fear of the Lord. It's a choice. Fearing the Lord doesn't mean being terrified of God but, instead, having a reverential fear of Him, loving what He loves and hating what He hates. It's coming into alignment with His thinking. It's taking the heart stance that I would rather do anything than offend His heart. He is our Abba Father. Abba signifies the close, intimate relationship of a father and His child, as well as the childlike trust that a young child puts in his "daddy." His arms are wide open.

Through uncertainty, discernment is found. Through brokenness, strength is found. And, through despair, hope is found. I have to be obedient to God's leading whatever that looks like to others. And, right now, it looks impossibly crazy even to me! This is going to be AWE-mazing, and I can't wait to see where it leads!

Chapter 13

The Diagnosis

◇◇◇◇◇◇◇◇◇◇◇◇◇◇◇◇◇◇◇◇◇◇◇◇◇◇

It's a normal Thursday morning to the rest of the world, but for me it's anything but a regular day. People are hustling to get to work and school, and the birds chirp happily, signaling a new day. The air is thick and muggy, and the sun greets me with an unusual brilliance. Clouds fill the sky while patches of blue peek through as if to draw my attention upwards towards heaven. Today is the day that I have been praying for since I was 17 years old.

I am filled with so many emotions that it's nearly impossible to define. The anxiousness engulfs me like a violent storm, but I am forced to silence the noise to make the solo drive to Charleston, South Carolina. Luke offered to go to the appointment with me, but I can't handle the stress of hearing my test results and dealing with a mindset that regularly questions the validity of my diagnosis. I feel the walls going up around me, which I know isn't right, but I can't find the courage to handle it any other way. I'm wrestling with trying to live a life of obedience to God all the while being in harmony with Luke. The last thing I need is to sit in the doctor's office and not be free to discuss my care while I'm worried about what my husband is thinking. I don't have the emotional energy to carry this dual load.

Feeling so lonely, I don't know how I would make it through, apart from Jesus. He is my refuge and strength, an ever-present help in times of trouble. His presence calms the storm just as

He did in the boat with the disciples. While the disciples were freaking out due to fear, Jesus was sound asleep in the stern. The panicked disciples awakened Jesus who immediately rebuked the storm then challenged their lack of faith. We can travel through any difficulty in life if Jesus is in the "boat" with us. I struggle with remaining calm throughout the entire "ride" but am growing more trusting each day. I'm not where I yearn to be but, praise the Lord, I'm not where I used to be! I want to be stable like Jesus and so assured of who I am in God that I don't have to explain myself. Jesus never defended Himself because He knew who He was.

I gather my multiple folders of past paperwork, doctor visit notes and blood work, which measures upwards of a foot if it were to be stacked up and leave for my appointment. I enter the highway heading south and distract my worrisome thoughts by turning on my favorite Christian radio station. Immediately, I hear these lyrics from my favorite song right now by an artist named Mandisa. It's become my theme song, if you will. I listen to it a lot especially when I am running, and it comes on so many times at the perfect time. This song is called "Overcomer," and the chorus is playing as if to send me a message straight from God:

"You're an Overcomer. Stay in the fight till the final round. You're not going under cause God is holding you right now. You might be down for a moment feeling like it's hopeless, that's when He reminds you, you're an overcomer."

Immediately, peace envelops me, and tears begin to flow. The raging storm within is silenced and my body softens. I know Jesus is in the boat. So much is riding on this answer today, and I'm kind of glad that I have a three-hour drive so I can talk to God about so many things. The quietness allows for clarity. I envision what may be ahead of me with treatment and cost and calm my thoughts with more music that encourages and motivates me. As

I near an exit that offers a needed coffee break and gasoline fill up, my phone dings with a text message from my youngest son. He recently got a cell phone and is only allowed to bring it to school or sports practices. Concern fills my mind that something may be wrong because he's in class and not allowed to be on it. Quickly, I pull into the nearest gas station and park my car closest to the double glass entrance doors. I take my phone out from the middle console and see that it is indeed from him because he is between classes. The message reads,

"Mom, remember 'Of all the people on earth, the Lord your God has chosen you to be His own special treasure.' I love you, Mom. Good luck."

Streams of tears openly flow, and there's no way I can stop them now. I don't want to stop them. I need this moment to feel the love and support from my kids who see a mom that's been through a lot and yet continues to persevere. I feel deeply loved and encouraged! I'm usually the one sending the texts or writing motivating notes, so this is new for me. It feels good!

We don't talk about all my illnesses as a family, but kids are smart. They see the pain behind the smile and know without really knowing how important today is to me. We don't have to walk the same road of another person to extend kindness, but we do need to slow down enough to put ourselves in their shoes. Showing compassion reflects the heart of Jesus. My youngest saw this verse on a special plaque hanging on our powder room wall and sensed the weight of its message.

All the heaviness in my body now leaves, and the tears give way to a big smile. I imagine feeling like the disciples did on that boat with Jesus once the storm suddenly stopped and gave way to calm. The fear and anxiety immediately leave. I am reminded of God's truth that He thinks about me non-stop, and that I'm highly valued as a special masterpiece. That promise is for everyone. Let that sink in a minute. We are valuable to God! The Creator of the Universe, the One who holds the stars in place with mere words, chooses us to be in relationship with Him.

I can feel the hope rising within me, and I am now ready to receive the news, good or bad, that Dr. Lieber shares. That plaque with the above verse from Deuteronomy 7:6 hangs in our bathroom to encourage others and remind them of their worth. I displayed it there for this reason. Today, it reaches deep down into my own heart and uplifts me. Children carry beautiful lessons if we carry teachable hearts. I am listening.

It's 15 minutes before my appointment time, and I am glad I am a few minutes early to gather my thoughts and pray. I need His peace especially right now because it feels like my stomach is doing cartwheels. I pull up to the front of the brown brick building and notice the other six or seven cars in the parking lot. I wonder if today is a "marked moment" for them too or just a regular visit and consultation. Can they too be waiting on an answer that's taken nearly 29 years? One car's license tag reads Pennsylvania and another Georgia. I see a couple South Carolina ones and one from North Carolina. I wonder how many people are here, if any, from other states requiring an airline flight? Dr. Lieber told me at a previous appointment that he's had people come from India, no less. His reputation precedes him, and I'm so thankful I am here. I trust him. He really seems to care about helping patients get well and not simply prescribing medications. He's not against medicine as needed but emphasizes the natural approach, and that aligns closely with my thinking and belief system too. These specialists are harder to come by, which is the reason that people come from all over the country and world.

I still cannot believe it's finally the day! A day that all these dots may get connected. A day that may change my life forever! I am ready so I exit my black Suburban and walk in to receive my greeting at the receptionist window.

"Can I help you?" she asks.

"Yes, I am here to see Dr. Lieber at 1:00 pm," I respond and give my name and paperwork. I find a seat away from the other patients in the corner of the small waiting room, facing the front door. To this day, it's still the position I am drawn to. I sit quietly alone with my thoughts then answer some text messages from friends and family wishing me well. Of course, one of those messages is from my parents who are two of my greatest advocates, cheerleaders, and best friends. Mom continues to support and encourage me throughout all the tears, indecision, anxiety, and turmoil. She's my human rock and don't know what I would do without her.

Time quickly passes and the nurse enters through the door calling my name to come back.

"How are you today?" she says smiling.

"I'm fine," I answer with the usual polite response. Actually, I'm a pit of nerves, but I will keep that to myself.

"Come right in here," she leads and directs me to the large conference room. "Dr. Lieber will be right in along with Dr. James. You are lucky to get both today. This doesn't happen very often."

"That's great, thank you! It must be a God thing," I answer. Now, I'm very nervous but also super excited. I get two great minds and only have to pay for one.

Not five minutes pass when the door opens and both doctors walk in to greet me. Dr. Lieber is in his late 70's while Dr. James is middle aged.

"Hi, Erin and welcome back. You look great, but I know that's not how you feel, so let's get started and go over these test results," Dr. Lieber announces. "This is Dr. James, and he sees patients here too. I want to introduce him to you today so in the future as I work towards retirement, he will be filling in more and more and may meet with you as well. Plus, you get both our thoughts, ideas, and suggestions today so that's a bonus."

As I greet Dr. James by shaking hands, I thank Dr. Lieber also and respond, "I appreciate both of you for being here to help me. I have a lot riding on today, and I believe God sent you both for a reason. I'm ready to hear anything you have to say and follow the advice you give. I just need answers!"

A short pause ensues and Dr. Lieber speaks up, "We have your answers after reviewing your IgeneX tests. This lab is the number one lab in the country for detecting vector borne disease, and the results are 100% reliable and true. I know you and I talked about the past testing you had which showed negative. This is the reason I wanted you to spend the money to have this panel done as it's conclusive and complete. Since you came to me back in February, and we worked on treating all your symptoms for perimenopause, gut imbalances, allergies, including the environment as well as food, and regaining health, I noted your overlap of symptoms. All of this makes sense now as I look at your blood work, and it will to you too. I know you've been waiting a lot of years, and I applaud you for never giving up. It's rare that we see patients like you that look this good but have these problems. You're an anomaly, that's for sure and definitely have God in your corner!"

I nervously nod as sweat beads on my skin and tears of anticipation advance. I feel that frog thing in my throat as I try to speak but can't. My heart is racing, and thoughts are circling. I wish Luke or my mom were here. Why did I come alone?

"Late Stage/Chronic Lyme Disease along with a co-infection called Lyme Hermsi (recurring fever) and mold toxicity," Dr. Lieber announces. "It's a high toxic load, that's for sure, but we are going to do our best to help you get well. You really are dealing with two big beasts, and for the amount of time you've been sick, it's going to be a process and not a quick fix."

Nervously but excitedly answering, I say, "So, is this why I have been declining so rapidly since I had that tick in my back three summers ago and never got proper treatment?"

"Absolutely," Dr. James responds. "You were suffering from what's known as Tick Paralysis meaning that your organs were shutting down. It could have killed you but, thankfully, you saw it and removed it when you did and received some days of antibiotic treatment, though it wasn't enough. Plus, going over your history, you have been sick for decades so it's hard to know if this diagnosis is the main driver or at least part. Therefore, it's such a difficult disease to treat as well as the mold component. We are needing to find out where these high mold levels in your blood are coming from also."

We spend the next 45 minutes going over the diagnosis and what all of this means. I am listening, but it's as if I am under water and everything they are saying is garbled and unclear. All I can think is how do I have Lyme disease when I am sure I was tested several different times. Is this what I suffered with since I first got sick at age 17? How long has this been the main driver of my chronic ill health? I remember having an actual tick in my back three years ago, but is that the reason I keep getting worse over the years? Why didn't the doctors for all these years find it and treat it successfully?

Despair and hopelessness flood my veins. Anger at how this wasn't caught storms my mind. I am furious at all these doctors over the years who made me feel like I was crazy and that it's all in my head! How dare they inflict their ignorance on another human being who simply was ill and didn't know why. It's shameful. All the looks and comments from them implying I needed to see a shrink. NO! I trusted doctors to know what they were doing and help me but instead I faced continual dismissal like I was some hypochondriac. This must change because no one should be treated this way, especially by the medical community. I did have some good doctors who listened and wanted to help but merely didn't have the answers as it was outside of their scope. I don't blame them. Those doctors spoke honestly, said they didn't know, and encouraged me to seek integrative doctors like Dr. Lieber. The system is the problem, and I feel exhausted from battling it for so long.

I am mad, and I'm not alone. There are so many of us falling between the cracks of what's covered by insurance and what isn't. How do you put a price tag on health? Our very life hangs in the balance of financial advantage.

Doubt, fear, anxiety, relief, and a feeling of being dropped into a deep dark pit inundate my soul. Why am I here alone? How could God allow this to go on almost three decades? Is this even still the answer or is there more? I don't know if I can process all of this. My lungs are closing in, and my breathing is shallow. How am I going to deal with four to five more years of intensive treatment and how am I going to pay for all of this? Luke is never going to believe me even with this proof because it isn't something like the "C" word that he understands and that mainstream doctors treat.

I'm happy I finally have a name but why, then, do I not *feel* happy? I almost feel worse. I feel like I'm going to throw up or faint or maybe both. Get me to my car and let me talk to Jesus.

He will calm my soul and help me make sense of all of this. I need to leave now. I barely hold back the stored-up tears, and I don't want to lose it here in the doctor's office.

Checking out at the desk goes as quickly as I can make it along with scheduling my upcoming visits over the next several months. I load my arms with supplements, vials of medicines, and all the information regarding what my life will look like for the next several years. I can't focus on anything else. My brain is on overload. I'm a wife and a mom with a daughter traveling for college soccer, a son about to graduate high school, and a 12-year-old involved in school and sports. Oh, and don't forget my two fur babies, a Cockapoo and Goldendoodle. I work two fitness jobs 20-30 hours a week and manage all the cooking, cleaning, yard work, carpooling, volunteering, and . . .

Deep breath. Deep breath. Deep breath. God help me! I can't do this.

I sit in the silence of my car, and it seems deafening. I turn the ignition key and drive to an isolated spot away from the other cars. I need to think. I need to pray. I need to cry. And I need to scream. Twenty-eight years of pent-up emotions burst forth like a breaching dam. I allow myself some time to sit in my pit of doom and gloom when suddenly a stream of hope floods my soul. It's like a new sunrise ushering in as it breaks through the fog. Prayer doesn't always give me the answers I want, but it does allow me to change my perspective. It causes strength to rise in me to meet the challenges ahead. Prayer is power to push through.

I had recently asked Mom and some close friends to pray for me because I felt like my hope was waning. This scared me so much. I started the year picking a "word of the year." It was a word that the Holy Spirit laid on my heart and would carry through the entire year. It's a word that keeps my mind and heart in the right place and gives me a compass of sorts. HOPE is my word for this year. With all the uncertainties and mounting discouragement, hope keeps me coming back to the foot of the cross. If hope is alive in my veins, God can show up and turn the situation around. It's life in my lungs.

Hope is defined as a feeling of expectation and desire for a certain thing to happen. There is a wishful type of hope whereas Biblical hope is not a mere desire for something good to happen. It is a confident expectation and desire for something good in the future.

"Do you not know? Have you not heard? The Lord is the Everlasting God, the Creator, and his understanding no one can fathom. He gives strength to the weary and increases the power of the weak. Even youths grow tired and weary, and young men stumble and fall; but those who hope in the Lord will renew their strength. They will soar on wings like eagles, they will run and not grow weary, they will walk and not faint" (Isaiah 40:28-3).

Deeper roots of hope are grown in running back to the cross. It's here that we can "Hold. On. Pain. Ends" (HOPE). It's like the baton handoff in the 4 x 800 track event. Holding on to Jesus in our difficulty leads to His renewed strength for our distress. The circumstance may not yet change, but our perspective and attitude will. I see it all differently now and realize I have a course of action; I have a treatment plan. I do have an answered prayer and that excites me! My circumstances have not YET changed, but I know what I am dealing with and can begin eradicating the disease and bring my body back into health! I see an answer to this nightmare, and I'm running the race as long as it takes. I must keep a marathon mentality and not a sprint mentality. I am fixed on finishing strong.

Chapter 14

Running On the Road Not Planned

Lyme disease is an illness caused by the bacterium *Borrelia burgdorferi*. These bacteria are caused by the black legged tick, also known as the deer tick. An infected tick bite under the skin can lead to infection. If diagnosed early, many patients recover. However, if not diagnosed early, Lyme disease can develop into a chronic illness that leads to long-term, serious health problems and reduced quality of life. In rare cases, Lyme disease can result in death.

Lyme disease continues to be the number one leading vector-borne disease, which refers to the transmission of a disease that is caused by a microorganism from one organism (the host) to another organism via a third organism (the vector). It's important to know the facts because it masquerades as other common illnesses and chances are you may encounter a tick yourself at some point or know someone else who has. While one is most likely to be bitten by a tick during the warmer months, ticks can be active year-round and are active at any temperature above 34 degrees Fahrenheit. Many people do not feel the tick bite nor get the rash. The highest concentrations of black legged ticks are found in the Northeast, Mid-Atlantic, and upper Midwest regions of the United States. In recent years, confirmed cases of Lyme disease have been reported in EVERY state. How many times did the doctors I saw write this off because they said Lyme wasn't in that state? Well, YES, it is. It is everywhere!

Most recent estimates are of 476,000 new cases of Lyme in the US every year. Scientists estimate that two million people could suffer from Post-Traumatic Lyme disease at the end of 2020. Lyme disease has also been found in 80 countries. Ticks look for hosts to feed – hosts can include pets, deer, mice, birds, squirrels, some reptiles, and yes, people. It is important to remove an attached tick as soon as it is found, and to remove it properly to avoid the spread of pathogens. Awareness, prevention, and early treatment are KEY. I surely wish I had this information years ago so that now I wouldn't be suffering like I am.

Lyme disease has been called the "great imitator." *Borrelia burgdorferi* can infect multiple organs and tissues, producing a wide range of symptoms. In its early stages, Lyme disease commonly results in a rash, joint pain, and headaches. Later-stage Lyme disease is characterized by arthritic pain, cognitive difficulties, fatigue, and other symptoms that can have an enormous effect on a patient's life. Lyme can mimic rheumatologic and neurologic conditions, as well as chronic fatigue syndrome, fibromyalgia, and many difficult to diagnose muti-system illnesses. Patients with longer lasting cases of Lyme disease may be misdiagnosed with somatoform disorders.

Testing. No testing is necessary when a patient has an expanding rash and a story that fits with Lyme disease. Testing at this early time is unlikely to give a positive result because it takes time to develop antibodies to the infection. Current tests sometimes fail to identify patients who do in fact have Lyme disease if testing is done too early or too late in the illness. A negative test result alone is not sufficient to definitively rule out Lyme as the cause of symptoms.

Common tests for Lyme disease include ELISAs and Western Blots. Both tests work by detecting the patient's antibodies reacting to the *Borrelia burgdorferi* bacteria. Many factors affect that response and the test's ability to measure it and can produce both false positive and false negative results. Although the CDC recommends a two-step testing process, consisting of an ELISA as a first test, followed by a Western Blot *only* if the ELISA is positive or uncertain, i.e., no further testing if the first step is negative, this testing scheme is insensitive. Additionally, positive results might reflect an old, rather than current, infection. Therefore, testing is only one part of the information that contributes to making the diagnosis. These tests have a high rate of inaccuracy of around 50% making it crucial to consult a Lyme-treating healthcare provider that can evaluate all your symptoms and medical history to make an accurate diagnosis (Global Lyme Alliance, 2022).

I took these two tests right after I had that tick in my back several years ago, and the results came back negative. I was put on a treatment course of Doxycycline which is the recommended CDC course of treatment for 20 days. However, Lyme specialist physicians recommend four to six weeks of treatment. I couldn't continue the medication due to severe reactions and side effects and therefore, stopped. Or, that's what I thought at the time. Knowing more about this disease now, I understand the reasons why I got so sick and couldn't continue taking the medicine.

When the treatment kills and releases toxins faster than the body can release them, it's called Jarisch-Herxheimer Reaction. Herxheimer or Herx Reactions are a short-term (from days to a few weeks) detoxification reaction in the body. As the body detoxifies, it is not uncommon to experience flu-like symptoms including headache, joint and muscle pain, body aches, sore throat, general malaise, sweating, chills, nausea, or other symptoms (ILADEF, 2022).

The antibiotic was doing its job to eradicate the bacterial infection I had and causing a severe die-off reaction called herxing. I didn't know what was happening, nor apparently did my doctor at the time, and no other suggestions were offered, such as getting proper detoxification support and replenishing important nutrients. I am now seeing how the dots are connecting and believe I suffered from Lyme disease since I first became ill at 17 years old. God is bringing a lot of my past illnesses together now with this current diagnosis.

So, here is the most important lesson I have learned: keep digging for the REASON behind the illness instead of merely accepting a symptom relief quick fix! And follow your gut and turn to God for answers! He will lead. Oftentimes, the Western medical system will cause us to question our sanity, and it is not in your head. That is what has been happening to me over all these years but, thankfully, I have ignored attempts at selling me a psychiatric diagnosis.

God will open and close doors. He never leaves us nor forsakes us (Hebrews 13:5) although He may shut down the "felt" presence. So often we obey only when we can feel His presence around us instead of thinking back to past places where He has been faithful in our life. Like Moses in reminding the Israelites of where God has taken them, we must look back in our life and recall the times He's been faithful. Find hope in those places of experience that if He did it then, He will do it again now.

I love the story in Acts 3 about the crippled man healed at the temple gate called Beautiful. The Greek word for "beautiful" is "horaios," which means the right time when things come together.

This man, from birth, was being carried to Beautiful where he was put every day to beg from those going into the temple courts. When he saw Peter and John coming one day to enter, he asked them for money. Peter and John did not have money to give but said, "But what I have I give you. In the name of Jesus Christ of Nazareth, walk." They carried the authority and power of Jesus. The man was instantly healed, jumping to his feet, walking, and praising God.

God's timing is perfect. He is never early, and He is never late. Often, we accept the lie that He has left us at the "gate," and nothing will ever change. It's our responsibility to keep coming with expectancy in releasing our faith for the answers to come. But what if our answers don't come today when we think they should? Wake up tomorrow and release faith again.

As with many patients who have multiple sclerosis, chronic fatigue syndrome and other chronic illnesses, many Lyme patients' neuropsychiatric symptoms are mistaken for mental illnesses, and they are prescribed psychiatric medications that they may not need. This Band-Aid approach may cover up symptoms and allow an active Lyme infection to cause ongoing damage. Like syphilis, Lyme disease bacteria can infect the brain and cause severe symptoms that may mimic clinical depression, anxiety, obsessive-compulsive disorder, bipolar disorder, and even schizophrenia.

Now, all the dots are connecting for me from the white lesions found on my brain years ago by my neurologist to these symptoms I struggle with currently. Because some present-day testing may be ineffective and inaccurate, it's important to step outside the Western medicine paradigm to get the proper specialty tests done and receive accurate diagnoses of the root cause.

Common symptoms of early Lyme disease include:

- EM rash (80% are solid-colored, and less than 20% have a bull's-eye appearance)
- Fever
- Headache
- Fatigue
- Muscle and joint pain

The non-rash symptoms are often described as a "summertime flu." Some people may notice areas of numbness or tingling.

Once the infection extends beyond the skin, it can affect any system of the body, causing symptoms that include:

- Debilitating fatigue
- Headaches
- Muscle pain
- Arthritis
- Numbness
- Tingling
- Nerve pain and weakness
- Heart problems
- Psychiatric symptoms
- Difficulty with thinking, memory, language, and math skills
- Problems with vision and hearing

When a patient is being treated for Lyme disease without success or is exhibiting additional symptoms that are not typically seen in Lyme disease, their health care provider should consider testing for *Babesia*, *Anaplasma*, *Ehrlichia*, and *Bartonella* (other infections that are often seen with Lyme). Left undiagnosed and untreated, these co-infections can not only cause symptoms of their own, but their continued presence can also prevent successful treatment of Lyme disease (ILADEF, 2022).

The test from IgeneX in San Alto, California also tested me for co-infections. I have what's called Lyme Hermsi or recurring fever.

What is Tick-Borne Relapsing Fever (TBRF)? It looks like Lyme, behaves like Lyme, but it's not Lyme. What is it? Tick-borne Relapsing Fever (TBRF) is a disease that presents very similarly to Lyme but is caused by a different set of species of *Borrelia* than those that cause Lyme disease.

How is Tick Borne Relapsing Fever Diagnosed?

TBRF can be fatal if untreated. As with Lyme disease, patients with TBRF are often misdiagnosed since the symptoms and signs of relapsing fever are relatively nonspecific. A Relapsing Fever diagnosis should be considered in patients who live in or travel to areas that are endemic for Relapsing Fever and/or experience Relapsing Fever or have Lyme-like symptoms but are negative by all Lyme disease tests. TBRF can be treated with antibiotics. Patients should be examined by their healthcare professionals. The healthcare professional will use clinical symptoms along with laboratory tests to discover a relapsing fever diagnosis or perhaps some other tick-borne infection. Scientists recognize more than a dozen tick borne diseases in the United States alone and new ones are still being discovered (IgeneX, 2022).

One tick may carry more than one disease, so sometimes people contract more than one co-infection from the bite of a single tick. The symptoms of these co-infections are often non-specific–such as fever and headache–which makes diagnosis difficult. And the treatments may be different. Doxycycline, for example, works for Lyme disease and Ehrlichiosis, but is not effective for Babesiosis.

Experienced doctors may be able to distinguish each of the tick-borne co-infections and order appropriate tests and treatment. Sometimes, they start to suspect a co-infection when the patient doesn't respond well to treatment, and it becomes obvious that something else is causing the symptoms. Co-infections generally result in more severe illness, more symptoms, and a longer recovery.

To conclude, Lyme disease is a complicated, multi-faceted disease which requires a multi-thronged approach to treatment. There is no silver bullet for late stages of this disease. No wonder, for all these years, I suffered as I did because mainstream medicine has not had the proper answers and ways of treating patients. Thankfully, more and more is coming to light which gives tremendous hope for others who are suffering like me. This will all be worth it one day when I come out on the other side as God promises I will.

Journal Entry
September 10, 2014

Though I'm most often focused on the physical side of it all, I also see how God is strengthening my spiritual and emotional health. Little things don't bother me anymore like they used to, and I appreciate the simplest of things. I notice the details of the flowers that catch my eye as I back out of my driveway, the brilliance in the leaves as seasons change, and the moments with those I love that bring light to my world. This is the part of suffering that brings gratitude. I am finding that writing down every day at least five things that I am thankful for is keeping my eyes fixed on the positive. This is so important to not get into a cycle of complaining and grumbling like the Israelites did. I am struggling with this mixed response, though, because it seems one minute I'm dwelling in the blessings and the next I'm murmuring about my troubles. God's angel army cannot go to work when we are grumbling and complaining. It's when we enter His truth and come into agreement with His Word that our angels can then go to work. There are three types of angel groups–warring, working, and worshiping. I know I need all of mine activated, so I am working to do better with not complaining, but it certainly is hard when you feel this awful. It's hard for me to know the difference between saying how I feel and acknowledging those emotions versus complaining.

I'm here alone in Charleston at Dr. Lieber's detox center and am very conflicted over this being a complete waste of time. I am supposed to be here for two weeks, but I'm not sure how long I'm going to make it. I have spent the day going in and out of the sauna, eating lunch, taking a couple of showers to rid my body of the toxins, getting further medical tests including an EKG, and receiving nutritional "cocktails" via IV. I miss my family, but I'm thankful that I get to stay with my in-laws and enjoy the nearby beach. I love how the Bible talks about Jesus regularly going to places of seclusion, and they come after both times of work and pain as well as times of celebration and rejoicing. He needed time alone with His Father, and I relate to this deeply. Getting away from the noise quiets my soul. God is always speaking if we learn to position ourselves to receive.

But I want to get my money back and go home. I miss my family SO badly! I feel that I'm struggling to maintain hope and that scares me. I've been disappointed so many times, and I can't seem to trust 100% in God's will yet fully for all of this in my life. It's even hard for me to be writing right now as I fight back nev-er-ending tears. I keep reading verses and devotions about "hope" because without that I won't make it. I feel like an 80-year-old trapped in a 45-year old's body. I'm so tired of the burden that pain brings and the inability to do life. I feel I have given up so much, and I'm not sure why this all is still happening to me. I can't catch a break. I can't get ahead of any of this. My whole world seems torn apart. I am mentally, emotionally, and physically exhausted. It's hard enough to take care of the family and household things when you can't even take care of yourself. I really feel like I'm drowning. I try to keep positive and go live my life in a "normal" way then some other illness derails me. I'm frustrated. I'm defeated. I'm sad. I'm angry. I'm lonely because no one truly understands. Well, of course Jesus does and without Him, I would be sunk. I must remember to keep Him in my boat and not keep freaking out in the storm!

I'm also so upset because my Run For God ministry started, and I missed the first two sessions. How in the world is God going to use me in this ministry when I'm engulfed with this treatment and how to cope with all of this? Thankfully, John was able to lead the first two weeks that I missed. He said they had to move the meeting from the regular sized classroom to the main auditorium because we had so many people–nearly 220! Holy cow, that's a ton of people! I am so excited that so many are showing up but how is this all going to work out with me leading when I still can't be there. God must have a good plan for all of this because it makes no sense to me. My prayer is *God, help me to do this right so You receive all the glory.* I need some victories, though, here on Earth! I keep feeling abandoned and gripped with human emotion, and I need to allow myself to run to my Father in Heaven and seek refuge in His loving arms. God keeps reminding me through reading scripture and listening to my favorite Christian songs that He loves me so much that He sent His only son Jesus to die for me. Sometimes, we must run away to be brought back to the foot of the cross and there we can be reminded of where we can seek our greatest place of rest. So, today, I am choosing God to be my haven, the place I dwell for help, relief, and rest. My heart longs to serve and honor Him, so my eyes stay fixed on Jesus. He WILL make all things work for good! He promises and He always holds true to His word. *Less of me and more of you, God. Dying to this flesh is painful and difficult, so help me walk in Your Grace today. I want to do it right.*

> "Be merciful to me, O God, be merciful to me! For my soul trusts in you, and in the shadow of your wings I will make my refuge until these calamities have passed by" (Psalm 57:1).

> "O taste and see that the Lord our God is good! Blessed is the man who trusts and takes refuge in him" (Psalm 34:8).

> "Dear friends, do not be surprised at the painful trial you are suffering as though something strange were happening to you. But rejoice that you participate in the sufferings of Christ so that you may be overjoyed when his glory is revealed" (1 Peter 4:12).

> "Therefore, do not worry about tomorrow for tomorrow will worry about itself. Each day has enough trouble of its own" (Matthew 6:34).

Chapter 15

Don't Stop Believing!

It's the last day of May, 2015, and it's been a long nine months of treatment, so this day couldn't have come at a better time! It's race day, and it's one that has me so excited that sleep last night evaded me. This isn't just another typical 5k race, though to everyone else showing up outside our group, it is. Today I am being honored by about 25 friends who are running to bring awareness of my Lyme disease in the local Chick-fil-A series race. I am so stoked that it feels like my heart could burst right out of my chest. It's an unexplainable feeling and that's saying a lot because I'm never really at a loss for words. I feel loved, honored, appreciated, encouraged, and SEEN!

When my friend Bev said that she wanted to organize a run for me and this disease, I couldn't believe it. I immediately felt validated for the first time in my entire health journey. It's like finally someone sees the "spots." I am used to doing nice, generous things for others with my time, finances, and talents, but I'm not good at being on the receiving end. However, I desperately needed a happy and meaningful event to help take my mind off what I am going through and that is what makes this such an amazing day. I don't like the pomp and circumstance towards me personally, but it's the idea that people care enough about what I'm going through to put a spotlight on the disease itself. That validation has me over the moon happy and encouraged.

Our lime green running shirts boldly state "BELIEVE" in white capital letters on the front with my declaration verse beneath it in smaller print. Bev chose these shirts for the group because it's my word and verse for the year. I am declaring and standing on this promise daily from Mark 9:23 which says, "Everything is possible for him who believes." The Holy Spirit put this word immediately on my heart as the expander to last year's word, "hope." Of course, hope continues to be important, but I'm challenging myself this year in my journey to "believe."

What does it mean to believe? We always live what we believe. I want my faith to be so strong that nothing can shake it. Like everything else in life, it takes intentionality and practice. The more we go through with God, the more history we build with Him. He remains the same. It's us who change. This allows us to see His faithfulness, ability, goodness, and willingness more and more, and therefore, release more faith. As I still race 10-15 races a year and continue teaching all my fitness and running groups, I face constant doubt apart from God's Word. Living in the "impossible" is the place I find myself in more times than not, and God keeps showing up in big ways.

Luke and all three kids are also coming, and the boys will be running. My daughter is getting over a soccer injury so is not able to run but will be cheering us all on. Having her here along with my parents is outstanding. This is the first time I feel Luke is outwardly supporting me emotionally, too, acknowledging why we are racing. He usually does his own racing apart from my running, so this is a big deal! This is the first time he's joining in a group race organized by friends of mine to highlight my illness. I can't stop smiling!

I love feeling understood by my husband. My mind reminds me often of the truth that Luke is doing the best he believes he can, but my flesh struggles to feel valued. I'm in a constant war within myself. Our spirit makes up 99% of who we are while our physical body is only 1%, yet it's commonplace to let our feelings dictate our actions. Our soul is our mind, emotions, and free will. It's how we think, feel, and choose. We are a spirit who has a soul and lives in a body.

"You were running a good race. Who cut in on you and kept you from obeying the truth?" (Galatians 5:7) Paul's reminder to stay out of confusion hits close to home. God is not the author of confusion. How do we get off course and distracted? It's when we take our eyes off Jesus.

During these last months of being on the Cowden Protocol has been extremely stressful. It's a natural remedies treatment created by Dr. Cowden, a Lyme survivor and specialist. Anyone having health problems can be on this protocol. The herbs are antifungal, antiviral, antimicrobial, and antibacterial. The protocol utilizes 14 different NutraMedix products taken rotationally. Dr. Cowden recommends staying on the program for six months but longer if autoimmunity is severe. Autoimmunity refers to one's own body attacking its healthy tissues making them unhealthy, thus creating illness and disease. Lyme disease and mold toxicity are in this category as they contribute to autoimmune disease just as my previous CFS, EBV have done. Basically, in layman's terms, the body is not functioning correctly. The root problem needs to be addressed in order for the other parts to work correctly and produce health. The body is a kinetic chain. One part affects another and so on.

My doctor and I decided that I would commit to one year and go from there. I take about 60 drops of different herbs in water four times a day and have to space my eating and meals out within a 30-minute window. My diet, again, is very strict, so I am eating no wheat products (gluten free), no dairy, very limited sugar, no corn and basically meats/vegetables/fruits. I have a paper booklet that lists it all so that I can manage. It's a huge time commitment and greatly affects my daily living. Going out anywhere is hard because my life right now revolves around all these herbs and restricted food and drink. I drink 14 glasses of water a day and have other supplements and injections from Dr. Lieber. I feel like my entire day is spent following this protocol because, well, basically it is! I am committed to this process that I believe God put directly in my path one day last fall as I was praying for direction. This door opened, and I walked in. I struggle greatly with the side effects of these herbs as they eradicate disease. I also make sure to do my infrared sauna treatments daily along with exercise. Running is highest on my list not only because I'm leading a running ministry but also because it allows me alone time with Jesus. It is my mission field. Every step brings new revelation and promise.

May is the month of shining light on Lyme Disease Awareness, and I posted often about this on my several social media sites, receiving great feedback. I believe it's my duty to share what I'm learning so that I can help others. God calls us into a kingdom purpose to live out here on earth. We are all given a sphere of influence. It may be in business, education, government, religion, or family. Living my purpose brings meaning and blessings to my life while planting seeds in the kingdom. Purpose fuels passion resulting in peace.

To think that a bunch of friends got together and put in all this work to honor me and bring awareness to Lyme disease blows me away! It's so nice to finally have a name that is somewhat recognizable in order for people to somewhat grasp what I, along with millions of people, struggle with. I share extensive facts to bring attention to this ever-growing epidemic. The more people see and hear about it, the better it will be for those in the future. I don't want anyone else to suffer the way I am. If God can keep one person from going down this same path, it'll all be worth it. People talk to me regularly about their health issues because they know I can relate and understand. Also, I want these years ahead of various treatment plans to help others as they too may need to navigate similar waters.

Like Paul, "I want to know Christ and the power of his resurrection and the fellowship of sharing in his sufferings, becoming like him in his death. Not that I have already obtained all of this, or have already been made perfect, but I press on to take hold of that for which Christ Jesus took hold of me. Brothers, I do not consider myself yet to have taken hold of it. But one thing I do: forgetting what is behind and straining toward what is ahead, I PRESS ON toward the goal to win the prize for which God has called me heavenward in Christ Jesus" (Philippians 3:10-14).

It's 7:00 am, and I arrive at the race site with kids in tow. Luke is driving his own car, so he doesn't have to stay as long. I need to be here longer to visit with my friends. Hugging those friends showing up is filling my heart to the brim. All of them raced my Run For God either this past fall or past spring and some did both. I love making these new connections through this running ministry especially as it's allowing me to connect with people from all walks of life and ages. While many attend my church, there are upwards of 8-10 different denominations represented, and I love that! God says He's not a respecter of persons, and I believe everyone should be brought into the fold. I feel like we are running advertisements to the other 150-200 runners and spectators here with these bright neon green shirts. Lining up for pictures, I surround myself with my family and thank them again for coming.

"I love you all so much and really appreciate the support more than you'll ever know! And, boys, you don't have to run alongside me. I'll slow you down, and you need to run ahead so you can get a good time," I say.

"No, Mom. This is YOUR race, and we are running with you!" they insist.

"I'm going to start at the front if that's OK," Luke says, "since the boys are running with you."

"Sure," I answer, annoyed.

The boys are ages 13 and 19, so it's extra special that they want to run with me, especially the older one because he runs cross country and track and is fast. The younger one says he hates to run, though he does for his soccer and basketball teams. He's not one to go run miles for fun.

Our large group gathers. As we prepare to start the race, I thank everyone for coming today and lead us in prayer, thanking God for the gift of movement and asking for His grace in every step we take. We line up side-by-side at the second row in front, and the gun sounds. We are off, and already I am doubting my finish. It's been a super hard week being on all these herbs and the effects they're having on my body. But I can't let everyone down because this is all for me! I talk to God and surrender my strength and abilities over to Him. My desire to win and compete at the highest level goes back to my youth and my performance driven attitude. I am competitive with myself and so often I wish I could come out to run simply for fun and not put so much pressure on myself. It doesn't matter if anyone else is even running; I expect SO much out of myself. I tell myself frequently that I have every reason not even to be walking let alone running and racing, yet I continue holding myself to the highest standard of excellence. Plus, I know God chose this path for me, and it's taking regular fleshly "drop-offs" to travel further down the narrow road. Proverbs 37 says that He gives us the desires of our hearts when we delight in Him. I know this heart's desire to run and use it for His glory is not by chance. I pray for balance and ask God regularly to change me from the inside out and take this desire away if it's not from Him. So far, it's ramping up and getting stronger!

Two hilly miles pass, and the boys are still running alongside me, talking as we go. I need water at the water station and a quick walking regroup so that I can make the final distance to the Finish Line. I see the lead pack charging the hill in front of us and signal to my oldest son to go!

"No, Mom, I'm not leaving you. I said I was going to run with you, and I am," he says.

"Honey, I appreciate you doing this and now it's time for you to go catch that lead group because you can win the entire thing! I'm good. Your brother is here. Go catch your dad," I laugh.

With the motivation he needs, he shakes his head, "OK," and sprints as fast as he can to catch his dad and others in the front group. He disappears quickly, and I then turn to the youngest as we are running again.

"You too need to go and leave me. I'm fine. I like running alone and need a few minutes to reflect. I appreciate what you did, now go run your race and try to catch your brother and dad," I say with a chuckle. There's no way he will catch them because they're super speedy, but it'll be fun trying.

He, too, disappears and now I am alone and able to talk to God and thank Him for getting me here today.

Approaching the final turn, I see the Finish Line about 100 meters away and begin to lengthen my stride with every bit of energy I have left. My face is flush from the exhaustion and heat. Though a 5k isn't long normally, today it felt like a marathon. But

I'm happy to see it's almost over as I hear cheers from the crowd lining the sides of the parking lot.

I hear my name yelled, "Mom, Mom!" and turn to see my youngest coming back on the course to finish alongside me. He already finished the race but spotted me coming down the final stretch. He grabs my hand in his and offers a few words of praise as I choke back tears. His heart grips me again today. He's such a great kid.

"Great job, Mom! Finish strong," he encourages as we cross together over the Finish Line, giving high fives to my parents, husband, and older son on the way in.

Walking into the medal the volunteer is hanging around my neck brings a huge smile to my face and heart. I did it. God did it. We did it. Nearing the coolers of bottled water, I quickly grab one and begin to drink. The heat is heavy, and my treatment is causing me to be hotter and thirstier than normal. Inflammation is at the root of my chronic illness, and it triggers more unwanted symptoms when the body heats up. I feel exhausted, drained, dizzy, and sick all over, yet I also feel exhilarated, excited, encouraged, and accomplished. I choose to live in the second atmosphere. The one that houses the spirit. It's here that feelings don't rule your life.

I am quickly greeted by my husband, older son, and daughter and am given big hugs and congratulations. Then, I head to the Finish Line again to cheer on all my other runner friends. This is the best part, getting to encourage and applaud their feat. Of course, my BRF Janet is here, and she finishes a few minutes behind me. I feel like a proud mama bear with her cubs every time I am here. To think that God chooses broken people like me to use in transforming other lives through running humbles me deeply.

All our Lyme runners are in, and we share stories of the race and await the awards. Scents of waffle fries and chicken nuggets fill the air, but I stick with a banana since I can't enjoy the other. It smells delicious, and I live vicariously through everyone else. As we sit on the curb as a family, I pause to again thank God for each one of them. I already won my prize. Their love and support charges my soul every day and, without it, I hate to think where I would be. They don't care if I win a prize, but I hope they see a living example of what it looks like to persevere at all costs. I hope they see a life running after Jesus is the very best one to have because it results in abounding joy despite difficulties or trials. My prayer remains that if God calls me home today, they will forever love the Lord thy God with all their heart, all their mind, all their soul, and all their strength. He alone is worthy of all the praise!

The last runner crosses the line and louder cheers ring forth amongst the happy crowd. The announcer begins to read the overall results and calls both my husband and older son to the stage to receive 2nd and 3rd male overall. Yes, the boy beat his dad even with me as his handicap.

"Great job, Son," I say, "way to come from behind and beat your old man! You could've won the whole thing had you not run the first couple miles with me."

"It's OK," he responds. "It was worth it!"

Deep down, I'm sure he would rather be taking home the number one spot, but I'm flattered and honored, nonetheless.

The announcer continues reading off the winner names and times, and it ends up including 15 of our running group! I won my new age group of 45-49 and masters overall. The prizes too are AWESOME! We are taking home umbrellas, hats, medals, and lots of coupons for future meals at their restaurant. That's a plus right there because we love eating at Chick-fil-A!

With prizes in hand and little pep left in our step, we say our so longs until the next race.

"Oh yes," declares Bev, "this is going to be an annual event so hang on to your shirts! Thanks everyone for coming out and supporting Erin and Lyme. I hope to see most of you at our next group run! Y'all crushed it today!"

I look around one last time at all the sights and smells and breathe it all in. I absolutely love race day. All the volunteers who come together to serve from a place of love and athletes of all ages, shapes, and sizes testing their fortitude for that day. No running race is the same just as no life race is the same. We all are here for different reasons. This could be my last race for a while, and I don't want to leave anything behind. I left everything out on the course again today, and that's how I want to leave this earth when it's my time.

"She gave it everything she had," is what I envision my tombstone saying one day. I'm not afraid of death because I know I'll be spending eternity with Jesus. But I'm not ready to go yet because God is just getting started with me. I remember making that phone call to my husband four years ago saying that I believed I either was going to die by age 50 or be rebirthed at age 50. I'm still a handful of years away, but I believe now that my rebirth is coming as I live out these challenging treatment years ahead. None of this makes sense, but I'm done asking "why?" and, instead, I'm asking, "what am I learning through this?" One moment at a time. Small steps lead to big rewards, and, in this moment, I vow to keep fighting no matter how long it takes. I believe God is who He says He is and that He will do what He says He will do. Today, I choose to believe.

Chapter 16

Live Forward

◇◇◇◇◇◇◇◇◇◇◇◇◇◇◇◇◇◇◇◇◇◇◇◇◇

God continues to show up at every corner and lead me through a new door of healing opportunity and this door at the Hansa Center for Optimum Health in Wichita, Kansas was one for sure. I didn't want to be in this situation of still needing treatment after these past two years working with some of the best doctors in the country who treat Lyme disease and chronic illness, but here I am. I finished the year-long Cowden treatment still suffering considerably and was told by my doctor that this illness, especially my "complicated case attacked hard by two doozies," was going to take a multi-faceted approach. It wasn't a simple fix. It was going to involve multiple years and multiple plans of attack to eradicate this difficult bacterium from my body, especially noting the longevity and complexity of my illnesses. Many people, he said, don't want to undertake this approach because it opens a can of worms that can be overpowering at best. It's very difficult staying on this course, but I am determined to see it through to completion or until God closes the door. Right now, He continues leading me to places like Hansa with fantastic opportunities, and I merely try to stay in step with what I feel He's directing me to do.

Since not receiving desired outcomes with the Cowden protocol, I immediately followed that treatment with a trip to Massachusetts where I saw another well-known functional medical doctor who also suffered from Lyme disease. It was a two-day appointment to be followed by at-home treatment under his care. He cured himself of the disease, so I valued his expertise. His name was Dr. Howard.

Functional medicine is a systems biology-based approach that focuses on identifying and addressing the root cause of disease. Each symptom or differential diagnosis may be one of many contributing to an individual's illness. I worked with Dr. Howard for only a few months. While working with him, my goals remained consistent: I wanted to get off all antibiotics for chronic sinus infections and have my gut completely restored. He prescribed different supplements to help with organ systems that weren't functioning properly and followed a similar path to Dr. Lieber and my other local doctors. He conducted extensive testing including DNA/genetics in order to give a better understanding of what my body was doing. The resulting treatment was comprehensive, essentially like having a full-time job. Thankfully, Mom was able to fly to Massachusetts with me for those in-person appointments, and we had fun touring the city on the days that I wasn't meeting with the doctor and undergoing therapy and testing. One of the great gifts of this disease is that the journey provides opportunities to be with people I love and visit new and fun places, creating great memories. The man follows in the footsteps of his mind, and I am learning to see and appreciate beauty in the ashes.

Once the three months ended with Dr. Howard, I came here to Hansa with the expectation of this being my last stop. Oh, how I've prayed this would be the final means to the end. The Hansa Center is an inclusive treatment facility where patients come to stay and receive various therapy modalities to heal from chronic conditions. It, too, is centered around the holistic approach to healing and wellness. Another friend of mine who has Lyme came here recently and told me about it. Since I was still significantly struggling, I began to pray for God to show me if this was where I needed to be. After thoughtful prayer, consideration, and working out logistics with finances and childcare, I ended up here in the hot summer month of August, 2016. Timing worked with the youngest being out of school and old enough, at 14 years old, to help with dogs and take care of the house. Also, my daughter was home from college and able to help as well. My middle son was away at Boot Camp on Parris Island, which proved to be a bigger emotional stress than anticipated.

Arriving in Kansas marked my first visit to this state. I experienced several firsts while there–first time being gone alone so long since becoming a mom 22 years ago; first time taking a taxi; first time depending on a shuttle driver to take me back and forth to treatment; first time feeling like a senior adult because the other three people riding in the van saved the front seat for me, saying they do that for their parents (I'm not that old for goodness sakes); first time walking to the store to get my groceries; first time being stuck somewhere without a car; first time biking to Target; first time walking to a laundry center; and, first time booking my own rental car for 24 hours so I could get out over the long weekend and not go stir crazy from all the other above listed "firsts."

I'll admit, I shed many tears once I arrived. OK, I was freaking out. The fear and anxiety gob-smacked me, and I had a full-on panic attack most of the day. It was an early Sunday morning and not having any transportation and being in a strange place feeling ill was too much for me. Treatments didn't start until that following day, and time stood still. I called Luke and talked to him a few times, but I knew I needed to get my attitude turned around and my head in a better space. Faith combats fear. I was overwhelmingly fearful facing this all by myself, especially when

I'm not healthy and not feeling well. It's one thing to tackle this stuff when I am feeling well and another when I am not sure by the hour if and how I am going to get by. At home, at least I have my family to help me with things but here it's all on me. Being in an unfamiliar environment can be distressing and unsettling.

I believe life is all about tests, and as a Christian, I know God will allow us to keep going around that same mountain until we pass. You never fail but, instead, embrace the opportunity to take it again as many times needed until character is refined. Moses told the Israelites, "Do not be afraid, God has come to test you, so that the fear of God will be with you to keep you from sinning" (Exodus 20:20). Prioritize me, God says, and pass this test. An intended 11-day trip resulted in the Israelites wandering for 40 years in the wilderness. When Pharaoh let the people go, God did not lead them on the road through the Philistine country, though that was shorter. God told His people that if they face war, they might change their minds and return to Egypt. Instead, God led the people around the desert road toward the Red Sea" (Exodus 13:17-18). Could it be that God takes us the long way through life because we simply aren't equipped to handle certain opposition? It's what's between the "Start" and "Finish" Lines of our race that can be messy. Life is about making it through the middle.

I went into these two weeks believing in my head that I would find success, but my heart was not matching up. Thankfully, that changed rather quickly as God started showing up in many big ways. The doctor was perfect for me, and I quickly learned to trust him. Dr. Garett was a Christian functional medical doctor. All the testing he performed aligned with previous testing, which brought me comfort knowing dots were connecting. Results were lining up with the symptoms, bringing me even more confidence. The Inn near the healing center was convenient for running and walking and even riding a borrowed bike on the adjacent golf course.

Treatment days included Monday-Friday from 8:00 am until 4:00 pm. I immediately met three new friends on the first day who also were staying at the Inn. I met two sisters, one from California and the other from Israel. Both had Lyme disease as well as their mother who had been treated here in the past. I also met a young mom of a two-year-old daughter from Florida. I could tell right away that God had me here not only for my healing but also to help with hers. She was at rock bottom with mold toxicity and Lyme disease. I had been in that similar place multiple times over the past couple years but currently was doing well energy wise. I believe God had me here to be an encouragement to her, her marriage, and home life.

"Focus on yourself while you are there because you're always encouraging and strengthening others," a friend said to me before I left for Kansas.

I ruminated on this as I entered day one of treatment and already felt called not to focus solely on myself. Upon meeting Donna, the one struggling so badly, I knew she was in a place I had been in previously and that I had the experiences and wisdom to help. I struggled with God for a bit wondering if I ever could come someplace and focus on myself. I didn't even get a full day before being confronted with this. After battling against my anger and selfish attitude, my spirit filled with the purpose that keeps me going. It goes back to the seed principle in the Bible. If we want kindness, then we sow kindness into others. If we desire love, then we sow lovingly into others. We reap what we sow. Healing comes when we help others. We were created to be like the Sea of Galilee and not the Dead Sea. One has an entrance and exit point while the other does not. Everything in the Dead Sea remains stagnant and dies because there's no movement; no life coming in and going out. Once we fill up, we need to pour out to others.

Donna and I became good friends, and I was able to get her a *Jesus Calling* devotional and a couple of other special keepsakes to help with her continuing journey. She was recently separated from her husband because he repeatedly questioned her mental competence, and the stress of her home being inhabited with mold overcame her. Navigating this is not for the weak at heart, and her support at home consisted only of her mother. It broke my heart because I understood deeply this painful road. Fortunately, my husband loves and stands by me even if I get angry and frustrated with how I believe he should emotionally support me. Many spouses in this similar place find themselves walking out on their suffering spouse and family due to the stress. That is tragic.

Dr. Garett and I had a great heart-to-heart talk during one of my hour-long appointments. Each day, I did the sauna for an hour, which gave me time to journal; rotated days with light and sound therapy; got an hour-long massage to remove toxins and other specialized therapies that targeted different organ systems in the body. We were served special green juices daily along with yummy electrolytes drinks. I brought my own lunch. My appointment times varied with Dr. Garett each day, but I loved that I got to meet with him personally as he provided different cranial and chiropractic treatments as well as herbal remedies according to how I responded the day before. The main reason I loved this place and wanted to come was for their belief that you don't have to experience all the herxing (die-off) to get better. They believe you should receive what your body is signaling it needs and, once given the remedy designed especially for you, you feel better. I will say that proved true. Though I never felt tremendously better,

I did get symptom relief in some areas, and Dr. Garett worked closely with me to dial in the others.

I especially recall one Tuesday at our 11:00 am scheduled appointment. The morning began early as I awoke at 5:50 am to get in a run on the golf course. The heat was already high at 72 degrees but, with the humidity, it felt more like 90-100. Dr. Garett worked extensively on my back the previous day and the back itself felt fantastic, but my hips, legs, and feet were burning, cramping, in pain, and weak due to neuropathy. Still, I was happy for some back relief because it loosened up, and I was not used to that. My energy was good, and my brain felt clearer and less foggy.

I loved coming into the main building to see the doctor because it was like being at a spa. The atmosphere was calming with soft music and invigorating with clean smelling essential oils filling the air. The employees greeted me with kindness and love. As Dr. Garett and I began working on that day's treatment, I had an important question:

"Now that I'll be leaving in a few days, how do I live my life when I get home? I don't think I know anymore how to listen to what my body is telling me regarding different pain signals because I've become an expert at telling it what to do regardless of the symptoms."

Pointing to the nearby chair, Dr. Garett signals for me to sit down.

"Tomorrow, I am having a 'Lunch and Learn' about the brain and its effects on health and disease. But one of the main key points is what you are asking me about right now," he says. "The hardest part for me as a doctor is getting my patients to live more in truth and not in fact. For you, it's the opposite. You learned how to live most of your life in the truth atmosphere and not the factual one of what your circumstances really are. Now, it's going to be a balancing act of getting the two to come back together."

"I know this sounds crazy, Dr. Garett, but I don't know how to do that," I answer.

"Make sure you come to tomorrow's talk as it will open new doors to your healing journey. It's going to be a key component for you in this process," he replies.

"It's not in your head, but it IS in your brain," Dr Garett opens the Wednesday 'Lunch and Learn' with. Wow! Now, that is a statement. How many times have I been called "crazy" and told that it's all in my head. Well, it isn't in my head BUT it IS in my brain. Interesting, I think.

Neuroplasticity is introduced, and it's my first time learning about this. Our brain is always in action. It's changing constantly. It is pliable. The brain is neuroplastic. It is NOT set. It's a use it or lose it machine. It's competitive. What we do to our body, we do to our brain. The brain and mind are different. The mind works through the substrate of the brain. The mind is what influences the body–nutritional status, hormonal imbalances, food allergies, toxins, digestive/immune/metabolic imbalances--all influences our mood, behavior, and attitude. Food is one of the most important interventions.

As a fitness professional and an athlete, I was taught to listen to my body. If there was any discomfort, signaling problems were looming, that activity should cease. I have often said, "Don't let your brain sabotage your body." We can't always believe everything we feel or think or every message that our body is sending because it may be in a limbic system trauma loop. These messages may be impaired from various stress responses. The limbic system is the part of the brain involved in our behavioral and emotional responses. It can often get "stuck."

Often, the term "mental health" has this crazy person stigma attached and that needs to change. Mental health concerns a muscle that needs tending to just like the rest of our bodies; neurology affects physiology and vice versa. The brain is a muscle that can become injured due to many variables, including bacterial infection like Lyme and mold but can be strengthened, revamped, and rewired with the proper tools. We are often hung up on labels and diagnoses without going to the root cause of dysfunction that can be corrected with accurate thinking, asking the "why?" instead of the "what?" Conventional medicine asks the "what?" while functional medicine asks the "why?" This is about creating health and not treating disease. Diet, environment, lifestyle, and purpose all affect wellness. Everyone is an individual. We are in an age of epidemic brain related diseases and disorders, and we each have the power to create change. Athletes may not even be aware of how critical the brain is to be strong and fluid in overcoming many ailments that may have originated in the brain. Our mental health affects us all in every way and is often overlooked as a vital piece of wellness.

I am learning so much about this muscle that is always in action, neuroplastic, ever-changing, viable, and competitive. It's a use-it-or-lose-it machine. Neurons that fire together wire together. Ninety-five percent of illness is either caused by or worsened by stress. I guess my past Duke doctors were on to something. Anxiety and depression are symptoms like so many other labels. They are real and powerful and can be reversed when looking at all the contributing factors. The brain is the optimal center for health and is very powerful. There are things we can do if we're willing to change our mindset and do some work. I'm leaving with new material to research and study as well as working on actual brain rewiring. I can wire bad out and wire good in. I love this!

The body can affect the mind. The microbiome links to many dysfunctions. The two are inseparable—one whole: one unit. The gut talks to the brain through the Vagus Nerve. The gut is said to be the second brain and second nervous system. Serotonin, a feel-good hormone, is 90-95% produced in the gut. The gut produces vitamins, digests food, regulates hormones, excretes toxins, and produces healing compounds. And, so, the gut is an important place to go with healing to combat many diseases and unwanted symptoms. This is one place I have been working on for years and am continuing in these current protocols. It's a ton of work, but I know it will be worth it in the end.

Preparing now to return home to "real" life, I feel like I finally turned the corner mentally and emotionally with the past 30 years of illness and searching for "the answer." I understand why God laid on my heart the word "resilience" for this year as it means having the courage to come back. I'm not feeling like I'm chasing after past help anymore but, instead, finally moving forward into a new life of wellness. I keep hearing in my mind, "Get up!" as Jesus instructed those who desired healing to do. We all get knocked down at times, and it's the ones who get back up who live victorious lives. We must live forward. Christians have no right living mediocre lives because the Bible says that Jesus died to give us abundant ones. Quitting is not an option. The best things take time to reach maturity. God is not in a hurry. We need to slow down and enjoy our life, which IS the journey. We are called to walk in victory. Victory requires power. And power requires peace. I am leaving here with a newfound sense of peace in my soul, one I've never experienced before.

Leaving Kansas, I can finally close doors to what's been causing my deterioration and enter the new ones that God opens. It's time to let go of all the baggage that's been weighing me down

– anger, bitterness, resentment, and hostility towards the doctors who didn't diagnose me properly nor treat me in a timely manner and correctly.

There are times to clear out the extra mental and emotional weight of the past. It's time for me to work on forgiveness to those I have been angry with including myself. I can now release myself from the understanding that I did all I could do to fight for what I knew I needed to fight for. We can't give what we don't have. I'm not responsible for what I don't know, but when I do know better, then I must act better.

I am leaving with a newfound courage. I feel the Lion of Judah roaring again within me, and that is amazing! I see hope in every turn. Dr. Garett says that I have an 80% chance of all symptoms disappearing within 45 days. He says that it will be like I wake up one day and it's gone. It may be a slow taper, or all symptoms may go at once. I will ask myself, he says, what did I do differently yesterday or this week and there won't be an answer. Everything will merely have come together producing the desired results. That is what God promises in Ecclesiastes 3, "Everything has a time and season, and everything is made beautiful in its time!" We can't be on mile 26 of the marathon and quit before the final 0.2! What if our miracle is on that last two tenths of our life race? What if it's the last quarter of a sports game, and we're down by several points? There's time left to turn it around. If I'm alive, God is working, and He's not done with me yet. I say out loud nearly every day, "God is doing a miracle in my life" even when it hasn't manifested yet.

I stand believing that I am healed and will continue taking the remedies and supplements as suggested. I know my journey continues, and I resolve to remain steadfast and joyful apart from circumstances I may continue to face. The Bible tells us to renew our mind daily, set it, and keep it set. We do it on purpose. Decide to push through and enjoy life even if on paper there is every reason to quit. Showing up promotes change. I am so thankful for this time that I received treatment but, most importantly, I am thankful for the healing for my weary and worn soul. Life at home has been stressful with constant disagreement centered around my healing journey and being here was exactly what the doctor ordered. These two weeks changed my life forever. Not much changed as far as my physical health goes, yet my soul sings a new song today. No matter the physical outcome, I press on, forgetting what lies behind and moving towards a new beginning that lies ahead.

> "Forget the former things; do not dwell on the past. See! I am doing a NEW thing. Now it springs up; do you not perceive it? I am making a way in the desert and streams in the wasteland" (Isaiah 43:18).

I SEE it!

Chapter 17

Answer in a Box

◇◇◇◇◇◇◇◇◇◇◇◇◇◇◇◇◇◇◇◇◇◇◇◇◇◇

I was running my weekly Sunday morning sunrise Jesus run at my favorite college campus. This is my happy place! I began talking to God about organizing another Run For God session. With so much uncertainty regarding my health, I wasn't sure that I would physically be able to tackle another long session. I asked God for clarity that Sunday morning and didn't get a definitive answer.

It was a damp, rainy morning, and I was rushing to get my desired miles in and get home. It seems it's always a mad dash Sunday mornings to run before church, but it gets my week started off right, so I make it a priority. Flying into the house and heading up the stairs, I see a somewhat large rectangular box sitting on the hallway rug.

"Luke, what's this box for?" I asked as he sat in the nearby room. "And it's all wet from the rain and how come it's delivered on a Sunday? Nothing comes on a Sunday. That's weird."

"I have no idea," he answers.

Knowing I didn't order anything and being rushed to get ready for church, I left it where it was. I never thought about it until I received a phone call Monday afternoon while sitting in my son's school carline.

"Hi Erin, this is Carol from Run For God ministries. I'm calling to let you know that your 10 devotional books should

155

have arrived or be arriving any day now. All the contributors receive 10 free books to keep or share as you wish."

"Hi Carol, this is Erin," I say. "I don't mean to sound stupid, but I have no idea what you're talking about. What do you mean by contributor?"

She continues the conversation, "You being a contributor for having your story as one of the devotionals published in our latest *DEVOTIONS 3* book."

Still completely confused and now chuckling, I respond, "Wait a minute. You're saying my story is in a devotions book?"

Now, I remember hurriedly writing a summary version of "My Story" as I waited for my husband to get ready for a concert. I literally wrote no more than 10 minutes and never proofread any of it. That was weeks ago. Several Run For God friends had seen that the new *DEVOTIONS* book was coming out, and they were taking submissions and encouraged me to send mine. So, I had a few minutes that one night and quickly wrote out whatever came to mind. I hit "submit," but it never went through (or so it said). I saw the "try again" message at the bottom of the screen as Luke came downstairs to head out to the concert. I figured, oh well, it's not meant to be, and closed out the screen. I never thought about it again until this call.

I proceed to fill Carol in on these above details, and she breaks out in a full laugh.

"I promise you I had NO idea that this went through let alone was published," I laugh. "God does the craziest things with me regarding answering my prayers, so this shouldn't surprise me."

I filled her in about my prayer that Sunday morning, and she was in awe as well. I figured she probably thought I was nuts, but it's how God and I roll. She continued laughing but in the best of ways and answered,

"Yes. This is the right Erin Leopold."

Still in awe and still chuckling, I reply, "What is my title, and what page am I on?"

"Your title is 'Running Redefined,' and it's on Chapter 31!" she says.

"OK! I hope it makes sense," I respond. "Now, I can't wait to get home to see what I wrote!"

My son and I scurry home to open the box with the 10 DEVOTIONS books. How crazy is this?

I grab my reading glasses so the print is clearer, snatch the book, and open to Chapter 31. Then, it hits me again–another AGT! The chapter number is 31, and I immediately think of Proverbs 31 Ministries and the recent writing conference I attended and the Proverbs 31 woman who seems to have it all together. Nothing happens by chance. There are no coincidences. In God's economy, everything happens for a reason.

I got my answer for leading another session as well as a bonus of further sharing my story in print. I ran with that too and landed in a local running magazine spotlight as well as making it to the top 100 contestants for *Runner's World* cover story. I didn't get the cover but making it to the top 100 proved exciting and motivating to continue the journey of healing through running and helping others along the way.

Destination Charleston Marathon, here we come!

Chapter 18

Everyone Has a Story, What's Yours?

◇◇◇

Arriving in Charleston right on schedule, I am feeling all sorts of ways. It's 4:00 pm and the first stop is at the expo where my Run For God (RFG) runners will pick up race packets and any other information needed for tomorrow's race. The race packets include the runners' bib number and other goodies like pamphlets to local restaurants, discount coupons to various places, and trial size energy bars. Because this is a large race, it's a big event with a bustle of activity coming in and out. Race sponsors are here with booths displaying their products like sunglasses, food fuel, and massage services. I love this part of the process because being amongst all the runners heightens my enthusiasm to that next level. Being the coach and leader, I don't run in the races we attend as a group. But, I am still responsible for making sure all of my 32 runners get what they need to arrive at the Starting Line tomorrow prepared and excited. This group had 44 runners total throughout the 20 weeks but not all are coming to participate in this race. Some wanted to do the program simply for the strengthening of their life race as well as getting in better shape and others chose to stay behind and participate in a local race instead of incurring the cost and drive.

I hated leaving the way I did having yet another disagreement with Luke about everything, it seems, happening in my life. We still aren't on the same page with the ministry I'm leading regarding the sacrifice of time and energy it is for me. I know that I should weigh in more on his thoughts and opinions but when it's clear that God is calling me to do a ministry like this, I'm not willing to be swayed by someone else's perspective. It's not that I don't value his opinion, but at the end of the day, I answer to God alone for the choices I do or don't make. Obedience is fundamental. So, I pray often asking God to show Luke why I'm doing what I'm doing even when it doesn't make sense to our natural minds. This is the ongoing crossroads we face.

The Bible says that God calls many but few are chosen. The chosen seek to walk the narrow road and it's often misunderstood by others who travel the wide path, the Bible calls it. It's a choice to surrender to God's obedience or that of man's opinion. It's our job to say "Yes" to God when He calls us into something and then pray for others around us to receive it with open hearts. First, we come humbly making sure it's from the Lord before we eagerly ask God to change everyone else. I just wish He'd change Luke first, but that's not the way it works. *It's so hard doing this dying to the flesh stuff!* I feel like I am still misunderstood when what my husband sees me doing doesn't match up with how he sees me trying to cope with my illnesses and treatments at home. At home, I am able to let my guard down, feel the heaviness of how I truly feel physically, not having to put on a brave face. And honestly, I still don't blame him one bit, though his attitude keeps me perpetually frustrated and upset. I can't say I'd be pining sorrowfully over someone when they're still doing all this activity and taking on so many things. I'm the one living in duplicity between two atmospheres, and that spirit realm cannot be understood until the Holy Spirit causes eyes to see or ears to hear. And, heck, I can't even explain it, and I'm the one going through it. We can't put

God in a box of human understanding. The mysteries of God are just that…mysteries.

One of my pastor friends graciously reminded me how important it is to keep a balance and proper alignment with God, spouse, family, church, and others. There's so much tug-of-war happening in my life right now, and I'm really trying to do what I feel led in my heart to do. Yet, I know things are not in proper balance. I'm so busy trying to survive these treatments, take care of everything regarding the kids and household as well as my part-time fitness job, and lead this ministry God's called me to. Daily, I weigh the burdens of guilt against God's filter of truth and desire to do it right.

This pastor drew out a visual representation on a piece of paper in bubbles of spheres and influence. God is the number one position followed by your spouse, family, then church. I believe a vast majority of people, including Christians, seek to fill that "God spot '' by desires of the flesh but nothing can and ever will fill that spot. God designed that opening for Him alone to fill. I believe that many people spend their entire lives chasing hobbies, fame, fun, addictions, and even worthy things like work, health, and family but only God can fill that number one spot. He must be first and Lord over every area of our life for us to be at rest.

I'm shifting over these thoughts as I greet some of my runners and their families pulling in the parking lot to get their packets and visit the expo. Quickly, my attitude changes for the better, focusing on being here now and enjoying this race weekend. And not only am I thrilled to be leading and coaching, but I'm also privileged to have my youngest son here with me helping out, allowing us time together. Having family with me is icing on the cake, and I treasure these moments whenever I can get them.

Leaving the expo after about an hour, we head to my in-laws' house about 30 minutes away. It's always great catching up with them over dinner and conversation. After eating a yummy meal of salmon and sweet potatoes, I gather all my poster boards, markers, and supplies to make cheering signs for the morning. It's time consuming but so very worth it. I know when I'm racing, I love to see signs that people are holding up. Some are funny and some are motivating. Either way, they're a great addition to the overall racing experience.

"Look Up Child" by Lauren Daigle rings out on my phone alarm and I scramble to locate it, acknowledging my distaste for a 5:00 am wake-up call. Because I hate to be rushed, especially when I'm the one in charge, I'd rather pad in some extra time than cut it close to the wire. With gear and supplies in hand, my sidekick and I head out to meet our runners. Parking is easy this time of morning, thank goodness, and my assistant is quiet but jovial. Even though he's a teenager, he wakes up happy and goes to bed happy nearly 100% of the time and is so fun to hang out with. I'm truly blessed.

As runners and families congregate after making that final porta potty stop, the dawn of the new day is breaking. The air is thick and cool now, but it's going to be a warm day for January. I welcome each one as they gather around and give last minute praises and hugs. Butterflies fill my gut as if I were running today. I love these people so much and the opportunity they entrust me with. Running is a wonderful teacher, revealing who we truly are. It teaches us to live beyond our feelings in a place that demands intention. Sometimes, discovering our weaknesses and flaws can be ugly as we simultaneously discover the beauty of our strengths and attributes.

Many of these runners were friends before this session started but some came as strangers and quickly became friends. Some of the athletes participated in at least one or more previous sessions and came back specially to train for this longer distance one. Janet is here, running her first marathon in memory of her dad who passed away recently. She has a laminated photograph of him pinned to her jersey. Others are running for personal reasons with tributes like hers on the back of their shirts. This is one of my favorite things God laid on my heart to do when I first started this program–design and wear our own race shirts instead of the official Run For God ones.

"What's Your Story?" it reads on the back of our royal blue performance wicking shirts. Between the two sentences is a big white box reserved for their story. My graphic designer friend printed the shirts, and she had this brilliant idea when I said, "Wouldn't it be neat to have people write verses or something funny or motivating, whatever they want, on the back of their shirts so that people can have something to read while they are running for a couple of hours?"

I thought: what a great way to spread the gospel as well as having a special part of themselves displayed on their backs. The idea was a huge hit, so we use these shirts for every race. Also, I can locate my people much more easily amongst the large crowd of runners!

The runners take time the week before to decorate their shirts with all kinds of colored markers, fonts, and even pictures. As they pray first over what message to write, it becomes a highlight of the session and fun for all the runners. The kids especially love decorating theirs. Once they're done, pictures are taken and sent to me, and I share on our social media page. It heightens anticipation and excitement for the pending destination race. Tears are shed as I read each one as well as laughter at the comedic ones and fun memories I recall. I pause in each moment, reflecting on that person's story, and it reminds me that we all have one to share. Everyone goes through ups and downs, and it's how we run our life race that determines our failures and successes.

Words have power and bear fruit in our life. The Bible says they bring life or death. We want to speak life and hope into all those weaving lives with ours today. Like me, those who do multiple Run For God sessions often buy a new shirt each time to write their story anew since life is fluid, and our stories are constantly being written. Since no one really knows what another person is going through, these shirts offer a glimpse into their life. God wants movement not perfection.

A few stories on the back of our runners' shirts today read:

> "Doctors said I might lose my leg. I said my running days were over. God said, I'll see you at the Finish Line. I can do all things through Christ who strengthens me" (Philippians 4:13).

(This male runner is early 30s and had a mountain biking accident that caused a large part of his quadricep muscle to be cut out. Doctors gave very little hope of walking much less running. He is here, trained up properly, and ready to prove them wrong and show the power of God).

> "But as for you, be strong and do not give up, for your work will be rewarded. 2 Chronicles 15:7….
> By PERSEVERANCE the snail reached the Ark"

"Running my first marathon in memory of my Daddy! (Name inserted and dates). In Christ there is still JOY in sadness. 1 Thessalonians 4:13-18 I'll see you again Dad! 1 Thessalonians 5:16-18 Rejoice Always"

"Running for a Cause, Cause I'm CRAZY!!!! And addicted to Running, and THANKFUL that I can...Thank you, Jesus.... Now Cheer LOUDER! I'm Pooped!"

And mine: "CHOOSING not to be defined by limitations. EMPOWERED by a living God BIGGER than anything on paper. 30+ years fighting Lyme disease and chronic illness. #RESILIENCE"

The front of our shirts has a half circle image of runners with a large, tall cross and under it reads: Everyone Has a Story. "And let us run with perseverance the race marked out for us, fixing our eyes on Jesus" (Hebrews 12:1-2).

I love this passage in Hebrews, especially all three verses, but we didn't have room on the shirt for all of it. It's our themed signature verse, if you will, and says,

> "Therefore, since we are surrounded by such a great cloud of witnesses, let us throw off everything that hinders and the sin that so easily entangles and let us run with perseverance the race marked out for us. Let us fix our eyes on Jesus, the author and perfecter of our faith, who for the joy set before

him endured the cross, scorning its shame, and sat down at the right hand of the Throne of God."

It's divided into three foundational parts:

1. "Cloud of witnesses" refers to the faithful ones gone before us, our ancestors, those who by their testimony encourage us in running. It's looking to those people now or ones who have passed that shines greater purpose on making running not about us.
2. "Throw off everything that hinders and entangles." This refers to sin. In our life race, it's about getting rid of things in our life that don't honor and glorify God. In running, we refer to unnecessary clothing or items that slow us down. Or, our entanglement can be emotional or mental baggage that we need to check at the door.
3. "Fix our eyes on Jesus" speaks to our life's race, continually going back to the cross and keeping Him in the position of first place. The Joy was His prize that enabled Him to endure suffering on the cross to pay our sin debt in full. In our running race, we keep our eyes fixed on Him for the strength and endurance to see it through to the finish and keeping that goal as the motivator to press on through challenging moments.

The group gathers for final pictures and prayer.

"Dear Father, we thank You for this day that You have given to each one of us and the opportunity to use this gift of movement that we call running. We ask for Your strength to fill our lungs with each step we take and endurance to see the race through to the very end. Help us to mount on wings like eagles and run and not grow weary. Shine Your favor on us to be the salt and light amidst the waves of runners today. Allow our stories, the testimonies of our life to speak love, hope, and joy to all runners we encounter today. I ask for Your blessing and favor to go before each runner here today and for You to equip them to run the race marked out for them keeping their eyes fixed on You. Let them run THEIR race and no one else's! You, God, are the God of BIG things undefined by logic and reason so cause us today to expect the impossible. Show up in ways we could never write for ourselves, and though it may be hard, encourage us to stay the course and not give up. Champions are those who keep getting up no matter what comes their way, so may we run our race today focused on the real prize of honoring and glorifying You in each step we take. We love You, God, and thank You for allowing us to gather today to run. We run for those who can't and wish they could. Movement is a gift, and we are grateful for it. In Jesus' name we pray and praise, Amen."

Chapter 19

Run With Perseverance

◇◇

All the runners are called to line up, the National Anthem is sung, and the horn sounds signaling "Go time!" The half marathon group and marathoners stagger the start by 20 minutes and soon the starting area is clear of runners. The course makes its way through the well-known Battery area, through downtown, finishing in the northern part of the city. It's a point-to-point start to finish, so we all rush to our cars and make a mad dash down Interstate 26. My youngest son and I arrive at the finishing area and find a parking place along a quiet neighboring street, gather our waters, camera, poster signs, and bag full of items needed for what will be another six or seven hour long day. I am extra nervous today because four of my left foot toes appear to be broken after I carelessly ran into a corner wall in my home two days ago. I was carrying a full basket of laundry which clouded my view. I misjudged the distance of my turn from the hallway into the kitchen and crashed my foot into the wall. It was so loud that my son heard it in the adjacent room. I was in a lot of pain but didn't have time to see the doctor. I did call the office and speak to the nurse. She advised me to come in for an X-ray based on the description of the swelling and bruising, but I informed her that I didn't have time and would come after this race weekend. I was quite confident that they would put me in a boot, hindering my ability to lead the way I desired–very hands on! I kept this incident between my youngest and me because I didn't want to hear Luke, other family members, or my group runners trying to talk me out of going. I prayed for God to lessen the pain enough for me to bear and allow my focus to remain on my runners and not myself. I was NOT going to miss the big event that we had all trained so hard for!

There is a band on the final corner turn before reaching the last 100 meter straightaway to the Finish Line. The music heightens the excitement and energy for the spectators and runners who are mere seconds away from their accomplishment. Different area high school bands are taking turns playing lively music. It's like one big dance party!

I am super proud of each half marathoner and hug each one coming into the finish, briefly hearing highlights and lowlights from the race. A couple told me about other runners on the course commenting to them about how much they loved our shirts! This makes my heart so happy and full! The half marathon group did an incredible job, and we got pictures of each one as they made the last tenth of a mile stretch to the Finish Line. All my runners met or exceeded their time goals: an extra bonus! Their training, hard work, and dedication paid off.

After watching and cheering for all the half marathoners coming into the finish, it's now time to start making my way to different checkpoints to cheer on my marathoners. Running on sheer adrenaline, I begin making my way to the mile markers on the map where I can see most of my runners coming through. Because they all run at different paces, it's tricky planning, but I've been doing this so long, it's like second nature. I leave my boy back at the finish area so he can take pictures of any others coming through and with the families from our group. Plus, I usually end up running some of the course with runners who are struggling and need some motivation, and he isn't into doing that. He is doing such an incredible job with this new lens and camera he got for Christmas. He's been excited to try it out, so this was the perfect occasion to do so.

As the weather heats up towards mid-morning, I wish I would've remembered to pack shorts and short sleeves. These black training pants are fine to spectate in but way too hot for actual running. I find several great spots near water stations to see a large majority of the group coming through, and I cheer them on, asking how they're doing. I also take some pictures to share later. I'm handing out water as needed, retrieving warmer clothing no longer needed, and taking down any other information they are giving me. So far, everyone is holding up well until I see Janet coming, indicating she has a migraine headache. It's not uncommon for her to have migraines but not usually during race days. I can see she needs a hat or sunglasses to block out the glare, and thankfully I have extras in my duffle bag. I also have extra gum and energy chews along with other helpful items my runners may need.

Backpack in tow, I begin running with her as well as her youngest son. She is hurting and afraid of the migraine worsening, forcing her to quit. I am now drenched in sweat from these hot clothes in the 65-degree heat, and the broken toes I sustained are screaming for help. I am in pain with the toes as well as having neuropathy and back pain. Sciatica is acting up, the dizziness is full on, and a headache ensues. My energy is low due to the taxing medical treatments, and exercise draws out the pain and malaise more. This scares me, but I know I can make it because God has continually pulled me through over these past years. I know He'll do it again. We have history. I tell my runners often that it's the same with God and their running. The more time you spend in relationship with Him, the more experiences you'll have to reflect on and note how you made it through. He is faithful.

Praying quietly to myself, I continually give it over to God because on the course helping my runners is where I'm needed and the place I want to be. They probably can get through without me but since I'm not able to participate like them, it's a blessing to share some of this journey with them.

After running with Janet for several miles, I log another five or six total between all the going back and forth on the course and mile markers. I am feeling poorly, but I can't let anyone know because it's their day. I have to put my problems aside, and I do.

Around noon, many of the marathoners make that final run down the shoot to victory! Families are cheering for their loved ones, and my heart fills with each one coming across that Finish Line, arms in the air, praising Jesus! It's an amazing sight, and I still can't believe God chose me to be the recipient of this blessing. I don't know how I would be getting through this misery I'm facing without this group. They are my lifeline but don't even know it.

Suddenly, word is delivered to me by some of my finished runners that Betsy is not doing well physically. She is one of my runner friends who did the Chick-fil-A race to raise awareness for Lyme disease. She began having difficulty around mile 12. Some fellow runners had stopped and helped with Tylenol and fluids and, with her insistence, they continued their race.

"Where is she on the course?" I ask the two runners that were helping her around the halfway point.

"We aren't exactly sure, but I'm thinking she's got to be around mile 20 if she's been able to make it. The heat is getting to her, and she is pushing through but needing help. She's very nauseous and chilled. I think Katie and Lisa are looking for her now," they answer.

"OK," I respond. "I'm going to see if I can find another one of our runners who may know more specifics." I find Bev, the one who organized my Lyme Awareness race, standing on the main street of the finishing area, talking on the phone.

"Erin, Betsy needs help. She's suffering and not sure she's going to be able to make the cut off," Bev says.

"What cut off?" I ask. "Oh gosh, I wasn't aware that they changed the official cut off time from 7.5 hours to 6.5 hours. That only gives us an hour, and I know how determined she is to finish this race."

Bev responds, "I'm talking to Lisa and Katie now. They found her around mile 22 and are getting her extra fluids and talking her through the pain. She's not doing well, Erin, and I don't think she's going to make it before the cut off time."

Immediately, my coaching gear downshifts to my Erin as a runner mode. I know I need to get to her because I'm the only one of our group who also suffers with these scary and unpleasant side effects and can evaluate the situation well enough to know whether she can be pushed more to finish or if a stop in the medical tent is warranted. Over the past five years running these races, I've experienced exactly what she's dealing with and more. I push my body so hard each race that dizziness and near blacking out is normal as well as chills, utter exhaustion, pain throughout my muscles and structure, disorientation at times, and overall feeling like death.

This is not to say, "Hey look at me and how tough I am." Instead, I am literally running in those shoes and still am able to finish the race. I know, it's stupid, and honestly, it's all probably not worth this torture I endure physically. Yet, it's what I'm embracing right now and not compromising to less than stellar circumstances. Somehow, it's the venue God is allowing me to use to heal the open wounds in my soul and grow closer to Him. I figure this is my life, and I'm not willing to sit around and waste it on wishing for better times. I can't be a spectator in my own life. I'll never accept this as my identity; I've learned to embrace where I am in the journey and seize every opportunity I have in life. While I'm working out my miracles with God and releasing faith for them, I must keep running my life race too until the breakthroughs come. And I know they will.

I don't know if Betsy needs more water, but it sounds like it, and I want to have as much with me as I can. All I can think about now is getting to her to assess the situation from my personal and professional standpoint. Working in Cardiac Rehabilitation during these past years and keeping CPR and First Aid certifications up to date, I can also evaluate her status from that perspective.

I hurriedly locate some water nearby and grab six dixie cups in both hands, three in each and fill as high to the top as possible without spilling over. Water in hand and exhausted from the day's events, I begin running fast enough to get to Betsy in time without running too hard spilling it all onto the heated pavement.

"Erin!" one of my RFG runners yells and steps closer as if to stop me. "You don't need to help because she already has Katie and Lisa out there helping her." This runner had created divisiveness in the group throughout the session, so this attempt at stopping me didn't surprise me. She may mean well, but I know in my heart what I need to do and the reasons for which I need to do them. I'm not sure of her motive but that isn't my business or concern now.

"I know," I answered. "But I'm going because it's what needs to be done."

With that, I continue my running pursuit in search of Betsy somewhere along mile 23 or 24. The heat is heavy, and my toes now are throbbing so badly that I don't know if I am going to make it.

God, please give me strength to keep running and get this water to her so she can finish this race. I feel so sick myself and I'm not sure I can make it, but I can't tend to me right now. I know You've allowed me to experience all this past suffering for moments like this when I can understand exactly what she's feeling. And I'm the coach and feel responsible for her and all my runners. Help me God. Help me. I cannot do this without You!

Shuffling my feet running against oncoming runners headed towards the finish, my phone begins to ring. How in the world am I supposed to talk on my phone with six cups of water in my hand? I chuckle aloud at yet another obstacle. With sweat pouring down my face and throughout my heavily clothed body, I stop running long enough to set down the water in one hand to answer the phone. It's Bev with a clock update.

"Where are you?" she asks.

"Coming into the back side of the park somewhere around mile 23," I say. "I don't see her yet, but I'm expecting to run into her at any moment. How's the time looking?"

"It's down to an hour!" Bev exclaims. "I'm staying here on the main street straight away where I can see the timeclock, and I'll keep calling with updates. You go find her and get her to the Finish Line before the cut off."

Pressing on with my run, thoughts are swirling as to what I will find. All I know is that she is going to make it if I have to help carry her across that Finish Line. This medal is important to her because it's a tribute to some close family members who have faced insurmountable circumstances recently and came out victorious.

Feeling the luxury of shaded trees lining the park's paved trail, I spot Betsy along with Katie and Lisa.

"Betsy! Betsy!" I yell and smile all at the same time.

Turning around, they locate me running ever so gingerly towards them as to not spill the remaining water. They all are walking, sharing stories, and Lisa is carrying Betsy's hydration pack. Betsy is visibly weak and overheated.

"Erin!!!!!" Betsy gasps with tears filling her eyes. "I prayed for God to send me His angels and give me wings to finish, and He did. They came and now you're here."

Assessing the situation quickly, because we are running against the clock, my no-nonsense personality kicks into overdrive as I pour the water on her head to cool her down. Her face is beat red and showing hot with her fair skin and freckled complexion. Like me, she's always been better at running in cool temperatures. The heat and humidity are not our friends.

Asking specific questions surrounding her issues, I ask, "Can you run? If you're going to make the cut-off time and get your medal, we've got to move NOW!"

"WHAT!" Betsy boldly declares. "You mean I'm not going to get my medal?"

"Nope," I say "unless we get moving now. We are down to the wire, but we WILL make it if we have to carry you across the Finish!"

Motivated instantly by that idea of going through all this pain and not receiving a medal, Betsy takes off running again to claim that prize she came for. She has that eye of the tiger response that nothing is going to stop her. With a renewed mind, she dismisses the last invitation to seek medical attention as we pass the last tent.

"I'm fine if you're holding me up. Let's go get my medal!" she exclaims.

With Lisa running behind carrying the equipment and extra water and fielding constant phone calls from Bev, Katie and I flank Betsy and scurry her along by the arms. By now, it's kind of in between a walk and a run, and we are literally holding her up by the arms. Running on sheer adrenaline and noting the time consistently on my watch, we continue walking and running over the next 20-30 minutes. We are losing track of actual time focusing on making this 6:30 cut off.

"Are we going to make it? Are we?" Betsy breathlessly asks. "I'm getting my medal!"

"How are you feeling?" I ask.

"I'm really thirsty and feel nauseated and super dizzy. But I'm going to make it." she responds.

Fielding yet another phone call and text and trying to keep Betsy going at the same time, I search frantically for that extra piece of gum I packed. All our water is gone, and I remember giving out all my gum on the half marathon course earlier today. Desperate times call for desperate measures, so I take my ABC gum from my mouth and pop it into hers. This is definitely going to take our friendship to the next level. Ha!

"It's a fresh piece." I announced laughingly. "Chew on this and focus on that and NOTHING else. All this other stuff you're talking about is causing you too much emotion, and you need all your energy for this finish."

The mind is a powerful thing and can take us to places we never thought we could go. We choose what we think about. Where our mind goes, we follow. Distracting her attention now away from seeing her family cheering on the corner and taking in all the emotion that results, I signal to her older son to come run with us.

Receiving the last phone call from Bev as we round that final straight away before coming into the last three turns to the Finish, it's like a movie playing out, and we are the main characters. Many of our crew are cheering passionately along both sides of Main Street as they see us coming. My mind is racing with focus and numbers, focus and numbers, focus and numbers.

"Are we going to make it?" Betsy wearily asks.

"Chew the gum. Focus on the gum!" I insist.

Having something to focus on that takes your mind off the emotional, mental, and physical pain is a strong tool. Gum is my go-to as it keeps the mouth hydrated and provides a means of allowing the brain to not overthink and over work. Of course, fresh gum is recommended but sometimes you do what you got to do. Thinking about something in this state is useless as the body is in survival mode, and it wastes needed energy. She is running on fumes, and the brain needs to stay relaxed.

I am so glad I am here with her and didn't listen to the one who tried to deter me. Now my coaching hat is on, and I know times, paces, and mileage like the back of my hand. *God, we've got this! Help us please to help get her across that Finish Line in time.*

The phone rings one last time as we now are in sight of Bev, "There's only three minutes left until the cut off. Y'all have got to hurry up!"

My heart pounds as I do another quick calculation in my head and realize we may not make it. *We ARE going to make this! I am near a 100 percent success rate with all my hundreds of runners I've trained over the years, and I am not about to fail now. God's got this. He's got us. I can feel His power made perfect in our weakness. It's as if we too now are floating as all my pain exits my body. Are we even running anymore? It doesn't feel like it.*

With Katie and I literally holding Betsy up and signaling her to continue moving her feet, Lisa and Betsy's son run behind. Glancing at my watch, I do another quick math calculation and pensively nod towards Katie to pick up the pace. If we don't, we aren't going to make it. We must speed up now! Katie sees the concern in my eyes and grabs Betsy tighter and says, "Hang on, girl! Your angels are getting you to that Finish Line. Look to your right. There it is, there it is!"

The band is playing another lively tune, and hundreds of people line the final turns to the finish. Focused and confident, I announce to the group, "When we get to this last final stretch, we are going to let her go, step off to the side and let her cross the line on her own!"

Everyone nods, accepting the plan. All our RFG runners are lining the last 100 meters shouting cheers and chants of "You can do it!" "You're almost there!" Spotting the clock for the last time and gaining that last burst of adrenaline rush, I see victory in the distance. We are going to make it! Looking to my right and left, taking in all the sights and sounds of this priceless moment, I declare, "Let her go!"

Betsy, with praise and worship arms in the air and a ginormous smile illuminating her face, independently crosses over that black mat under the Finish Line arch at 6:29:28! With 32 seconds to spare, that coveted medal was draped around her neck and immediately all the problems, obstacles, and pain disappeared. It was all worth it!

The crowd is ablaze with excitement and cheering. This is like a movie, and God knew all along how the ending was going to play out. This is really happening. Emotion seeps in and now

I fight back the tears of elation and anguish. Running 10 miles today wasn't what I planned for and yet, I made it. God is writing me into the story of the day, and incredible blessings flood my being. Chills form from my head to my toes, and all I can do is thank God for getting us here and allowing me to be a small part of their race today. It's as if God winked at me, saying, "Here you go. I'm blessing you for blessing them."

Taking a moment alone, I bend at my waist resting my hands on my knees, catching my breath, quieting my soul, and thanking God for sending Betsy his angels. The RFG family gathers around our determined and celebrated champion of the day with acts of kindness only shown by those with hands and feet of Jesus. Jesus was all over this course today, and I'll take this memory with me for the rest of my life. Some say it's "just" running or it's "just" a race. I say, "Yes," it is, apart from inviting God and His supernatural power to come alongside. He was welcomed here today, and we expected Him to show up BIG! I can honestly say that He blew it out of the park!

Soaking in the calm after the storm, I pour one last bottled water over Betsy's head to cool down her red beating face and hot body. Isn't this the perfect picture of what Jesus does for us every day. He washes over us the peace and rest of who He is. He is our Living Water and invites all of us daily to come to the well.

As runners congregate sharing stories and tending to other's needs, Bev laughingly comes over with an announcement. "Guess what? A few of us found out after my last phone call that they extended the time by an hour because of the heat!"

Only God can write a story like this!

Chapter 20

Run to Win

"You WILL Win!"

It's a typical muggy September day and the breeze ushers in a bit of relief from the high humidity and rising temperatures. It's my favorite time of year, leaving summer behind and entering autumn. I love Charleston, but I could do without the humidity. Beginning my six-mile run with ear pods in place streaming Christian contemporary music on Pandora, I circle Waterfront Park before ascending the half mile 5.6-degree slope. This is the heart rate kicker and then it's smooth sailing down the hill into town until it's time to turn around and head back again.

The winning words spoken by Dr. Henry yesterday echo loudly and confidently in my mind as I prepare to meet with Jesus on the Arthur Ravenel Bridge also known as the Cooper River Bridge. She is overseeing my care now since Dr. Lieber retired. A running event takes place here every spring, and it's still a family favorite to participate in. But, days like today are the best because crowds aren't gathered and it's time for me to meet with Jesus alone. Jesus often withdrew from crowds to meet with His Father in the morning while it was still dark (Mark 1:35). Praying at night or early in the morning, on a mountaintop, or in a desolate place allowed Jesus to give His full attention to God. The Gospels tell us that He often sent the crowds away so He could pray. This is a spiritual discipline I didn't start out practicing but rather embraced as a means of craving time away from the noise. God is always speaking, but are we always listening? A person can hear individually from God in all sorts of ways. Running with God is my worship and therapy!

I schedule the meeting with Jesus as often as I am in Charleston. Since it's usual for me to run the first morning I am in town, I don't waver. I don't ask myself how I feel. I just go. I am addicted to The Holy Spirit high and can't go too many days without it. I am suffering greatly with pain related to my body detoxing on this antifungal medication. My muscles always feel burning tightness. Neuropathy still fills my body with episodes of stabbing pain down my legs and into my feet. This morning is extra hard because I cried most of the previous evening in pain.

It's hard to be away and not in my own home so I can wander from room to room and be alone in my grief. Most nights now I sleep upstairs on the third floor so I don't disturb my husband's sleep with my tossing and turning and crying out to Jesus. God doesn't cause suffering to teach us a lesson, but He does allow it to grow our character. As a Christian, the Bible tells us that we are to put on our new nature in Christ and take off the old. The Holy Spirit is the mediator, and the mind is the bridge (Ephesians 4:22-24).

The God meeting is planned to begin 30 minutes before sunrise, and all I need to do is show up in my running shoes, bringing an expectant heart and open mind. Music is optional. Some runs, I relish in the quietness of the new dawn listening to what's on God's heart while other times I fill my soul with motivating lyrics or encouraging podcasts. Today, the inspirational tunes are playing.

Dr. Henry is now working with me on my new year-long mold protocol, and my mind fills with yesterday's takeaways.

Mold is the underlying piece of this massive puzzle affecting my health. Many people who can't seem to get well are often told it's the Lyme, EBV, or other related viruses or infections and yet the largest fire to extinguish is mold toxicity. Mold toxins are the #1 culprit keeping mast cells and the nervous system on high alert. A mast cell is a resident cell of connective tissue that contains granules rich in histamine. Mold toxicity weakens our body and throws the immune system way out of balance. It's the domino effect from here, and quite probably at the center of many existing struggles.

Going into moldy spaces, I become unable to function neurologically. My chest tightens, making breathing shallow and labored, dizziness ramps up, confusion and delusion sets in, and stabbing throbbing pain fills my muscles and joints. It's very frightening. Generally, I hide it and act like everything is fine, but, at times, it overtakes me to the extent that I must leave where I am and regroup somewhere else. While it's my normal, I don't accept it, but I do embrace it. There is a difference between the two. Embracing allows us to acknowledge the validity of something while accepting is receiving something to be correct. I make this distinction because it keeps my identity distinctly apart from my struggles. Yes, I have these circumstances, but I do not come into agreement with them because they are not of God.

Disease is not from God but results from this fallen world. There is no sickness in Heaven, and my prayer often is "thy Kingdom come ON EARTH as it is IN HEAVEN!" The Lord's Prayer says that we have to bring Heaven to Earth. Oftentimes, I break out into terrible anxiety and uncontrollable crying before I enter a room or building or encounter certain chemicals, scents, or food smells. My body basically goes haywire. This is known as nervous system dysregulation.

Even drinking water on certain days causes my nervous system to over respond. Taking over-the-counter medicine like aspirin is still a challenge and this is the reason I have worked hard for over 30 years to find and treat the real underlying causes so that I can live a normal healthy life. I'm another step closer now to identifying this root cause.

Dr. Henry and I looked over my blood results, and she pointed out the three very dangerous levels of molds in my system. "These three are government approved bioweapon agents similar to Agent Orange, and they're in your system," she explained. "It's a miracle in and of itself that you're even walking, let alone doing all the running and activities that you are. People with these agents and levels are much of the time disabled and unable to do simple things."

The anti-fungal treatment we decided on is less toxic to the body than other similar medications and supposed to be lower in adverse side effects. It does give me headaches and produces burning and cramping in my lower extremities especially while running. Thankfully, this is a prescription medicine covered by insurance and is considered a very safe drug which is used with young children and nursing moms, so I agreed to go this route as my body couldn't handle antibiotics anymore.

I am now 18 months without any antibiotics, which is a first for me in over 25 years! God and I are working out my first big miracle! Many people think they have sinus infections like I did when 93% of them may be fungal infections.

Cresting the hill and looking out over the dimly lit water, cargo ships are slowly coming into port. My body is spent from the climb and breathing is labored and heavy. Physically, I am already worn but, mentally and spiritually, I'm coming alive. Words of encouragement, peace, and motivation fill my ears, and thoughts continue regarding my conversation yesterday.

"How are you doing?" Dr. Henry asked.

Again, being overtaken by yet another hot flash caused by a mast cell spike, I reply, "I'm OK, just a bit overwhelmed today at all the pain I live with and things ahead of me that I'm facing."

As she gently put her hand on my knee, she said, "Erin, you CAN do this!"

Fighting back the tears, I responded, "Well, I really can't but I know God can give me all that I need to make it through, and He WILL! This year I'm focusing on the word 'miracles' because I believe this is the year for them to show up!"

Smiling and affirming my decree with a nod, she leaned in closer making direct eye contact, paused in a commanding posture, and said these words, "YOU WILL WIN!"

Catching my breath and turning my legs over quickly to allow for the downhill fun, my thoughts are turned to these three powerful words. It's like stepping back into "the zone." We as athletes get our minds set and bodies prepared for the task at hand and it's vitally important, as Christians, that we do the same thing. Coming into this appointment with Dr. Henry, I was out of the zone, but I returned strong as she spoke those life-giving words. Receiving them and believing them put me quickly back into the zone and into the game. The mind is the battlefield. Many times, we feel fearful, alone, discouraged, angry, disappointed, hopeless, or rejected and, therefore, take ourselves out of God's zone. Meditating on the Word, declaring His promises, praying, and worshiping OUT LOUD are ways to quickly get back into the right zone. When words are spoken aloud, the brain receives the information three times greater than if one simply thinks the thoughts. From this place, we are more than conquerors the Bible tells us because we fight FROM victory to victory (Romans 8:37). It was all done for us at the cross, and we merely need to receive it by grace through faith. Jesus paid our debt in full! This is the love zone where we find God. He is perfect love. He is the same yesterday, today, and tomorrow.

Finishing the run and reentering the park, my body yearns to rest while my soul sings of His new day's mercies. My body screams, "I'm done!" while my soul shouts, "Keep going!" I wasn't supposed to be here today because of changed plans yesterday, but I stuck with Plan A because I knew this is where I am supposed to be. The run changes me. I'm not the same person leaving as I was starting. Something transformative happens, and I go away stronger in spirit and stronger in soul. Mental, emotional, and spiritual health are just as important as physical health.

The God meeting closes with ponderings of the miracles so far this year. God never ceases to blow me away with His faithfulness and goodness. Many say God is good when things turn out positive, yet I declare God is good ALL the time.

Chapter 21

Eat to Win

◇◇◇◇◇◇◇◇◇◇◇◇◇◇◇◇◇◇◇◇◇

One exciting healing mechanism was obtaining my holistic nutrition certification to use myself as the guinea pig on this healing journey. Using food as medicine, I wanted to add this accomplishment, first for myself, and secondly for the people I train. This allows for a bigger scope of influence in my job and ministry. Three months of serious study, resulting in losing all my work due to a computer crash, thus forcing a complete redo in a shortened time, proved my will to be resilient and determined. No powers of darkness were going to come against me and stop me from adding this to my toolbox of answers. Of course, I had about an hour or two of a heavy meltdown, then regrouped and got it done. Success results in the number of times one chooses to get back up. The Enemy hates progress and promotion and will do anything to stop us. Don't let him!

Learning about food as medicine narrowed my already disciplined diet into a cleaner, healthier one by my choosing mostly whole foods that were plant-based. Eating clean is a discipline. It involves eating foods as close to its natural state as possible and staying away from foods modified with various chemicals. Clean eating means staying away from processed foods and drinks. Dr. Henry put me on a modified Stone Age diet eating mostly organic meats, vegetables, low sugar fruits like berries, and minimal complex carbohydrates. I became a voracious student of healing through nutrition and shared with my running groups, ministry groups, fitness trainees, family, and friends. Reading lots of books, listening to endless podcasts, and doing in depth studying through google, I used myself as the experiment for using food to heal. I don't get to be carefree and eat what I want when I want. I go to parties and eat ahead of time or when I get home. I hate ordering at restaurants, and I always seem to be the "picky" one. I don't like drawing this attention to myself or asking the half dozen questions about how the meal is prepared, either. However, that's the way it is, and I embrace it and make it work. I feel so much better eating more cleanly.

Inflammation is the leading contributor to all major diseases and reaches upwards of 10 times higher in people with Lyme, so deep diving into how to lessen my inflammatory rate is where I started. Posting a colorful anti-inflammatory food chart on my refrigerator guided my family and me into cleaner eating. Clean eating isn't about a diet but a lifestyle change, which begins in changing how we think. Swaps are one key to long-term success. Using good quality cooking oils like olive oil or avocado oil instead of inflammatory ones like canola oil or peanut oil are great swaps. Also, adding something each day like a high quality apple brings tremendous health benefits without giving up anything. Little by little, from glory to glory, we are changing so it goes with making better food choices. Be patient, and stay the course.

The saying goes, genetics load the gun, but the environment pulls the trigger. One of the things that we can control is our food choices. Many people aren't willing to do the work and take the personal responsibility to change their health by changing their diet and yet it can have a significant impact on overall health. God created us in a garden and though we live in a fallen world, we were created to eat fresh, wholesome foods. He tells us in 1

Corinthians 6:19-20 that "our bodies are a temple of the Holy Spirit and are not our own. Since we were bought with a price, we are to glorify God with our body."

We have a responsibility to take care of this temple including what we see, hear, and do. Medicines have a place for sure, but I strongly believe they shouldn't be the first go-to. Lifestyle changes with diet and exercise as well as reducing stress and getting ample sleep should be. Drinking water is also crucial! Our bodies and our minds are made up of about 70-80% water. Often, many health problems would disappear simply by adding ample hydration.

One size does not fit all. Not all foods considered 'healthy' work for everyone. Individuals are unique and wired differently. For instance, fermented foods are considered great for gut health but for people like me with significant mold toxicity and Lyme, it's contraindicated. I was eating these foods religiously until I realized these were the foods causing my uncontrollable itching. I felt like I had an army of ants living inside me from my head down to my toes. I'd lay awake every night itching for hours and begging God to take it away or give me answers. After about a year, I finally understood that some of the kefir and kombucha and some other foods were contributing to this problem.

For the past five years, my fear escalated when I had to drive to Columbia to see my daughter or attend other family outings out of town. I now can drive longer distances again without the severe dizziness and brain fog. Previously, I could feel fine for one minute and then eat a meal or go out into an allergy-ridden environment, and the symptoms would ramp up. With better nutrition, my energy overall is also improving. I experience fewer days of needing to take rest breaks, and my confidence is building again. Migraine headaches have disappeared, and other female infections are leaving. Breakthroughs are happening.

Miracles will continue to happen. I tell myself this regularly. I don't know how people survive without Jesus. It's not denying the existence of the problem but instead magnifying the power of God!

Chapter 22

Tearing Down Strongholds

As I run a last loop around the park to cool down, my mind again returns to strongholds and the power they have in our lives. Strongholds are anything that exalt themselves above God. They come from false ideas or Enemy lies and are designed to steal our focus away from God. When the Enemy wages war against us, the primary battlefield is the mind. This brain of ours is the control center of our body and how cool it is to reflect on that parallel of spiritual focus through mind transformation and bodily renewal through remapping and rewiring the brain. I am learning some areas in my life that are strongholds and need dismantling.

My marriage is one of them. I know in my mind that I need to let God handle my husband, yet I continue to get in the way of His working. It's a trust issue. God is calling me to a deeper trust in Him. It seems Luke and I are in a constant war of wills and decision making, and the stress is mounting daily. The house is having to undergo extensive mold testing and it's costly, not to mention, we both still are on different pages with our beliefs on how to deal with all of this. This is ordered by my doctors so I can be treated in the cleanest environment possible and yet all buildings, houses, and dwelling places, to some extent, have mold. My parents are even testing their home in case I need to stay there for a while. I'm trying to sort through having new HVAC systems

191

installed and the various companies are each giving differing opinions and recommendations. My home is chaotic.

I'm weary on so many levels. Luke and I love each other and are committed to our vows, yet I am struggling to walk in solutions of peace. My daughter is about to graduate college, and I'm trying to hold it all together for her and the family when I want to crawl in a hole and never come out. If I can't be in my own home because it's making me sick, where am I supposed to go? Or is this even the cause of my mold exposure? Answers are conflicting, and the fog is deepening. My emotions are ebbing and flowing like a giant roller coaster, and I feel like I'm losing it. I can't imagine living with me is very easy or fun. Episodes of crying hit me routinely, and it's all getting to me. Therefore, I escape to running in my happy places. Like charging my phone when the battery is low, my soul seems to need more and more opportunities of recharging.

Nearing my car and now feeling lightened in my soul and spirit, these words from Jeremy Camp's "The Answer" are playing in my ear pods:

"I know the answer to every question, the one solution to every fear. I know my helper where it comes from Jesus, He is the answer…"

Immediately, I pass this beautiful lady radiating joy, wearing a hat boldly displaying the words, "I Love Jesus."

Smiling really big I say, "I love Jesus too!"

Stopping, I share the words playing in my ears, and she quickly tears up.

"Thank you for sharing that!" she says, as we both continue on our way. As I finish the last several minutes of my run, I feel the Holy Spirit nudging me to go back and talk to this woman. So, I do.

"I feel like God is telling me to stop and speak to you so here I am," I laugh.

"My name is Erin."

Warmly smiling she replies, "I'm Maggie! I live close to here in Goose Creek. How about you?"

"Greenville, South Carolina," I answer.

We talk for a couple minutes sharing our stories and the mighty power of God in our lives.

"I have my own 53-year story," she exclaims. "I'm battling cancer now and have some important tests coming up on Monday. Can I give you my number and will you pray for me?"

"Absolutely!" And, as per my running "protocol," we take a selfie, agree in prayer, and exchange cell phone numbers.

"You know, Erin, those words you just shared with me that you were listening to are God's reminder to me that yes, He IS the answer!" Maggie proclaims. "You are my angel today. Thank you for stopping and sharing your story."

"So glad I did too, Maggie," I say. "You wearing that hat was my answer, and you today are my angel."

"And I am so sorry for making you stop your run," she answers.

"Not a problem at all! I am finishing up. I am here to worship today, and your hat reminded me that no matter what my circumstances are in all things, to keep my eyes fixed on Jesus!"

A few more tears are shed and we exchange hugs as I say so long and approach my car. Her smile and love radiated like a hot fire burning on a cold winter's day, and I wonder how many people today missed this opportunity to see Jesus. In five minutes of meeting and talking, I feel more connected to her than I do with some people I've known for years. As my sweat pools, I feel the same about the love pouring out of her onto me and others. I am so thankful I showed up today for my Jesus meeting.

"Do not forget to show hospitality to strangers, for by so doing some people have shown hospitality to angels without knowing it" (Hebrews 13:2).

Chapter 23

It Is Finished

◇◇◇◇◇◇◇◇◇◇◇◇◇◇◇◇◇◇◇◇◇◇◇◇◇

To the rest of the world, it's a regular Wednesday morning but, to me, it's anything but normal. Settling in from yet another trip to another specialist, this time seems different. I don't know how much more of this that I can take. I'm happy to be home, yet my home has become the place I trust the least. The new HVAC system is in place, but I'm still battling constant thoughts of mold being here, contributing to my illness and symptoms overtaking me every time I transition back from being away for a few days. My body is reeling from the plane ride which always heightens my neuropathy due to the vibration and altitude. My mind races with the new prescribed plan to treat me in these next two to three years. It's going to consist of more herbal supplements and an intense dynamic neural rewiring program for the brain. This program will require a year investment and take an hour each day to complete; 30 minutes in the morning and 30 minutes in the afternoon. The plan also requires that I live in an environment that is COMPLETELY clear of any mold, and I am not allowed to go into any buildings, including grocery stores and churches, that are older than five years of age. Basically, I am going to live in a bubble.

I need to have my home thoroughly tested again this time by one of the best mold experts in the country and also my parents' house in case mine doesn't meet the criteria so I can move

195

in temporarily with them. I love my parents dearly, but I don't want to live with them and leave my home, my youngest son, and my two fur babies. My mind floods with thoughts of this new life, and I feel deeply discouraged and depressed. I cry out to God regularly seeking answers to come quickly because I feel at the end of my rope.

This time, Luke attended the visits with me, which consisted of the usual two-day consultation and endless blood work and testing. We celebrated our 25th wedding anniversary recently and instead of going to Hawaii as he desired, we opted to make this doctor visit a getaway for the both of us. I want to go to Hawaii also but, in my condition, it wouldn't be any fun for me so why waste the money. We can go when this misery is over! All this already is costing a small fortune, and I'm thankful that God continues to provide through Luke in this area. I really appreciate this loving quality in him and can't say I would be as gracious if the tables were turned. My attitude would most probably be begrudging. I'm at the point in this endless journey of healing that I can't fake it anymore. I am worn down to the deepest level of my soul. I am happy that Luke agreed this time to meet with one of my doctors, and I felt like I needed him to be a part of my journey now since his mind is more open to what I'm dealing with. We are headed in the right direction. Dr. Pratelo is the doctor I came to see, a functional medical doctor who specializes in the treatment of Lyme disease. His approach is somewhat varied from my past doctors but is effective in eradicating this disease along with the Lyme Hermsi and mold. It requires a multi-systemic approach. This, still, is hard to get across to my husband, but I'm working on letting go of my control in trying to constantly change his mind.

God clearly told me that the only way I was going to win this battle was on my knees in tenacious prayer.

Some things in life come only by time and experience. When we are Born Again, everything God is becomes implanted in us in seed form. It takes a lifetime to grow in different fruits of the spirit–love, joy, peace, patience, kindness, goodness, gentleness, faithfulness, and self-control (Galatians 5:22). I am perpetually agreeing with God in the areas where I am weak and allowing the Holy Spirit to grow me. It's like giving birth to a baby. It takes nine months for the baby to grow before it is born. Self-control and patience are two of those areas God has brought to mind recently! Dr. Pratelo is certain that if I do everything he suggests that I will be completely healed of the disease and not merely in remission as past doctors said would happen. People come from all over the word to receive care from him, so I'm thankful for the opportunity to find one more approach to this relentless treatment course.

The flight to California was awful. Again, I got very sick on the plane fighting back the nausea and delirium. I recently learned that the vibration is what causes Lyme to flare up. My anxiety reached new levels and for the first day I couldn't stop crying and feeling like I was going to lose my mind. I sat awake the entire first evening preparing for my next day's appointment, sobbing uncontrollably, and arguing with Luke. He is calm and stable with his emotions and doesn't get heated until I keep pushing and pushing. It's then that all hell breaks loose as my stored-up anger and bitterness reveals its ugly head. It's like I can't help myself. Maybe I am going crazy? *I would hate to be married to me and put up with all this turmoil. I feel so guilty, but I can't help it. My emotions are out of control, and I'm working with God to heal so many wounds. I feel so sick and can't get ahead of any of this for any length of time. When is this EVER going to end? God, please take this away from me once and for all so I can have a shot at a better marriage and life.*

I truly want that for us. And, in the meantime, give me the grace to walk through it to bring You honor and glory. Less of me and more of You is my desire, but it is so hard.

I was able to calm myself down after talking to God and listening to some wonderful television preaching from Dr. Charles Stanley. The sermons I found pertained perfectly to my current situation, and it was again like God speaking directly to me! I love these prophetic acts where God speaks! Prophetic acts or markers can come through other people, sermons, music, billboards, street signs, something we read in a book or magazine or a host of other ways. Two of the most powerful ways He speaks to me are by His mathematical lingo and feathers. The Holy Spirit is everywhere all the time and causes everyone to see, hear, or feel uniquely individual things. While two people can experience the same event completely differently based on how the Holy Spirit speaks to them, it's so important to connect on that personal level to connect more deeply to God's heart and thoughts for us.

God desires relationship, not religion. As parents, we want the same with our children. He is our spiritual Abba Father. We don't have to figure out life for ourselves. We have the Holy Spirit to intercede on our behalf and direct us based on God's will for our life. Healing is in the obedience.

"I will instruct you and teach you in the way you should go; I will counsel you with my loving eye on you" (Psalm 32:8).

After our appointments, we went to some area landmarks in San Francisco like the Golden Gate Bridge and dined in some nice restaurants, so we were able to enjoy some of the trip. I didn't feel well most of the time, but I tried my best to have fun. It's not fair to Luke to have to listen to my constant problems. I get sick of hearing them myself, so I can't imagine what he must feel like. This is remarkably hard for both of us.

Catching up from our week away, I begin going through email, texts, and Facebook messages when my eyes catch an article written by a friend about being "addicted to the chase." The title intrigues me. As I read further, tears stream the contour of my face as I see so much of my life in this post about her story. Could it be possible that yearning so desperately for health is becoming a god in my life? I never thought this way before, but now I'm seeing things through a new lens. Isn't wanting health a good thing? How can it be bad to desire health? And, if I hadn't been pursuing all this would I even have made it this far and still be alive? With so many questions and thoughts swirling through my mind, I wander up to my daughter's room on the third floor. It's quiet here since she's away living on her own but all her childhood furniture remains. I need time alone with God to sort this out, and I feel a closeness to Him in this space of wonderful memories.

The gentle tears now morph into sobbing as I lay prostrate on her soft carpeted floor. No one is home so I'm able to express myself unencumbered and quickly these words come yelling out of my mouth, "WHAT DO YOU WANT FROM ME, GOD?"

Instantly, I hear the still small voice say, "I want ALL of you, Erin!"

"You have ALL of me!!!!!" I angrily scream and with that comes a surge of emotion that isn't stoppable. I allow it to flow as I extend my arms out on the floor in front of me, and I suddenly see and feel in my spirit the outstretched hands of God. My inner being calms and peace ensues. The anger leaves. I think this is an actual vision, but I'm not sure. This is all new to me. It's not scary at all but, instead, very peaceful and calming. It's as if He's grabbing me by the hands and physically holding me with His. I see Jesus in all white, angelic-looking, and I realize there's been so much that I have been keeping from Him. It's like this constant tug of war that's been taking place and now I let go of my end of the rope. He says He wants "All of me!" What does this even mean?

Praying continues until tissues are needed to mop up my emotional mess. As I stand on my feet, I see my daughter's *Jesus Calling* on a nearby shelf and pick it up to see what today's dated message reads. Maybe God is going to speak to me through something here. I've been asking God for a sign about continuing in this protocol set by Dr. Pratelo because the weight of its requirement seems unattainable. My marriage, especially, is holding on by a thread, and I know I cannot continue in this current path any longer. My brain aches with thoughts of navigating these next few years. I can't do it. Luke won't sell the house and, to be honest, I don't want to either, but I don't know what else to do. I'm like the dead branch on the tree about to snap off when the next strong wind comes along. I am at my final breaking point.

"COME TO ME AND LISTEN!" are the intro words to today's reading. Already, my heart is quickened as I continue down the page. "When I cried out from the cross, 'It is Finished' The curtain of the temple was torn in two from top to bottom. This opened the way for you to meet Me face-to-Face, with no need of protocol or priests. I, the King of kings, am your constant Companion."

As I sit stunned and quiet, the words, "It is Finished!" and "protocols or priests" ring loudly in my soul! This is one of the clearest revelations I've ever received and there is NO mistaking it's God speaking to me. As quickly as my mind reads these words again, I hear the Lord saying directly to me that it is time to end ALL my protocols and put my ENTIRE focus on HIM! *Seek My Face and not My Hand* I hear in my spirit.

His verdict is that I am healed!

I didn't know that the word "protocol" was even in the Bible and here it is right in front of me referenced on this page. I don't believe God could be any clearer and now my thoughts engulf me. I am terrified. How am I going to explain this to Luke after he just spent his time and money on this trip? How am I going to quit everything when I still have SO many symptoms I'm dealing with daily? How am I going to explain to him that I am healed, even though all my symptoms still manifest? I silence my mind, and "Trust Me" is the record I hear playing over and over and over. Like Peter who had grown tired from a long night of fishing with no success at getting any fish, Jesus appears to him and the other fishermen and says to go back out one more time and cast his net. Reluctantly, he does, and the net fills with more fish than Peter ever thought possible. It's a trust issue. It's a call to deeper waters. GO DEEP! It's a heart matter. I am scared to death. What if He doesn't pull through? Of course, He'll pull through because He is God and can't lie and therefore can't deny His own character. If God says He wants "All of me," then I'm ready to go ALL IN! I'm not even sure exactly what that entails except to dig into His Word and feast on His truths and promises. Obedience to Him is more important than my comfort.

> *God, please show me what You're trying to teach me through all of this so my testimony will point others to You. I spent so much time chasing the healing that I lost sight of chasing You, the Healer. Give me strength, courage, and boldness to fight the good fight and run this race until it's won. I don't understand any of this, but I'm choosing to trust You, even when I'm afraid.*

The day fills with more quiet time with God and me delving into scripture like never before. I search verses regarding trusting Him and begin writing many of them down to ponder and meditate on. If God wants me to trust Him more now that I'm out on this wobbly limb, I need to know more about who He is and what He says. I mean REALLY know! This isn't about a Sunday morning sermon or spotty devotional readings. This is going to a deeper place yet uncovered in my world. By nature as a fixer and problem solver, I land on Psalm 37 and write the first part of the chapter out by hand. This is going to be my recipe for healing in moving forward. I make a copy to keep in my Bible and one I tape to my bathroom mirror so that I can meditate on it first thing in the morning and last thing before going to bed. These are action words that I underline as they will lead me down my new path of growing in God's ways:

"TRUST in the Lord and DO good; DWELL in the land…"

"DELIGHT yourself in the Lord and he will give you the desires of your heart."

"COMMIT your way to the Lord; TRUST in him and he will do this…"

"BE STILL before the Lord and WAIT patiently for him…"

"REFRAIN from anger and TURN from wrath…"

Moses knew of God's ways while the Israelites delighted in His acts. I want to know the heart of God so that I can exit this wilderness and occupy my Promised Land. I am scared beyond comprehension and enlivened at the same time.

Luke arrives home from work, and my heart fills my throat as I prepare to share with him what God laid on my heart today. I prayed multiple times throughout the day for him to be able to receive this news in a positive way. If he doesn't, I don't know what I'm going to do. I must tell him that I'm not going forward with

Dr. Pratelo's recommended treatment plan, and instead, trusting God fully for my healing, starting with the brain. The doctor spoke so powerfully about neuroplasticity as my past doctors did also and so that's where I feel led to put my attention for now rewiring my brain! It's worth a shot.

Sitting down at the kitchen table, I say to Luke, "I've got something to talk to you about and it's important. Please let me say everything I need to say without interrupting because I don't want to lose my focus."

"OK," he says, pulling up the counter chair looking across from me.

"You know how God leads me in my life and how I try to obey that prompting? Well, He is leading me in a completely different direction than Dr. Pratelo is prescribing. I can't do what he wants me to do. I don't think our marriage can handle the stress and, to be honest, I can't live in a bubble and take all these remedies as he's suggesting. It's too much, and I feel like I'm about to have a nervous breakdown from all the trauma and stress. I spent time talking to God a lot this morning about all of this because I've been seeking answers since we were in California. I know we spent a lot of money on that appointment and the trip in general and that you went and supported me. And I really appreciate it more than you know. But God is telling me to stop everything and only work on the brain part of the protocol and focus my attention on Him. I'm not exactly sure what all of this means yet, I just know He keeps telling me that this has become a stronghold in my life, and it's time to let it go. I can't explain it any other way, and I hope you can support me in this as best as you can, even if you don't understand."

Pausing a moment to invite a response, my heart flips and flops as I take a deep breath and prepare for the worst.

"So, you're saying you aren't going to do any of the things recommended by the doctor we just paid all that money to see?" Luke questions.

"Yep, that's right. I don't expect you to be happy or even understand. I just need you to know that I KNOW deep in my spirit what God spoke to me through the words I read in today's *Jesus Calling* and try your best to support my decision," I acknowledge.

I proceed in sharing the details of the "It is Finished" and "no need of protocols and priests" to him stating that those three words let me know I was done with treatment as I knew it. I am healed! And, I explained that no more protocols were in order nor seeing any more doctors on a regular basis. "Priests" immediately suggested doctors. I didn't need to continue with any more protocols recommended by doctors. I am finished.

You could hear a pin drop as I finish my explanation and try to read his body language. I can tell he's not thrilled to hear this news but, also, he's not mad. Luke takes longer than me to process emotions and doesn't wear them on his sleeve like I do. Men and women are wired so differently, that's for sure!

"OK, I hope you know what you're doing and it all works out the way you want it to," he says.

And, with that, I end the conversation because I'm learning that Jesus never explained himself to others and I want to be more and more like Him. I'm good with this response. I know what God is saying and that's all that really matters. Now begins the final chapter of this nightmare for me with a new confidence to trust Him fully and step out. God's got my back!

Chapter 24

Now I See

◇◇◇◇◇◇◇◇◇◇◇◇◇◇◇◇◇◇

I was led to EMDR therapy by another door that God opened for me when I began my quest to heal my brain last year. There, He directed me to stop all supplemental/remedy treatment for Lyme/mold. EMDR therapy stands for eye movement desensitization and reprocessing, an extensively researched, effective psychotherapy method proven to help people recover from trauma and other distressing life experiences, including PTSD, anxiety, depression, and panic disorders. I read books on the brain by Norman Doidge, Caroline Leaf, Annie Hopper, John Sarno, and Daniel Amen to name a few. As I sat on the beach one October day reading about the divided mind, I learned about this therapy and its effectiveness in treating PTSD. I quickly recalled what a good friend, who happens to be a therapist, told me years ago after my traumatic back surgery in Florida when I clearly suffered post-traumatic stress. I filed that away as "life kept me too busy to sort through any of that" and recently began to acknowledge the truth of my wounded soul. Working with Monica in EMDR the past four months taught me that I never took time to process my emotions like David did throughout the Psalms. That was a huge eye-opener for me. I would experience an emotion or feeling and basically take it to God in prayer and say, "You've got it," and carry on to the next thing. I never paused long enough to filter my feelings through God's truth in the Bible. I was a master at stuff-and-suppress and now I am working to dredge it all back up so that I can get to the root problems and heal my soul. How can anyone go through decades of infections, illness, and conflict without suffering from post-traumatic stress? Isn't that a term reserved for people coming back from war or survivors of sexual abuse or something like that? I learned that it absolutely is, but that it also covers ordinary people like me who have endured decades of pain.

I also remember a doctor friend telling me about 15 years ago that I could juggle it all for now but by the time I reached 50 years old, it would all catch up with me and bury me if I wasn't careful. Approaching age 50 in a few months has me convinced there have been no truer words spoken. And, as I read those pages that October day, I stumbled across a section that listed a website for EMDR therapists in different states. I knew right away that I needed to find one. I literally called from my beach chair and scheduled an appointment for when I returned home. At my first visit, Monica said, "How did you hear about me?" Glancing at the notes and displaying a big smile she said, "Oh yeah. You found us in a book on a beach sent by God!"

With a giggle I replied, "Yep! I know it sounds crazy, but God sent me, so I know this is where I need to be." God owns the blueprint for my life, and my race is unique and unlike anyone else's. Other people can't hear my wind; only I can.

Elijah is a great example of getting in position to receive what God had promised (1 Kings 18). There had been a drought and God told Elijah to go with his servant to the top of Mt. Carmel and get in position first to be able to receive the promise of God; he was believing for rain. Elijah stepped into the promise by releasing his faith that the rain would come because God said it would. The servant went seven times and saw nothing, and

Elijah told him to "Go back!" Finally, he saw a cloud as small as a man's hand. That was only a small bit of evidence that Elijah acted on. First, he believed. Second, he got in position by getting his chariots ready. And, lastly, he ran ahead. Elijah became afraid of Jezebel, who threatened to kill him, and he ran for his life. He went alone to the desert and hid under a broom tree and prayed that God would take his life. He was defeated and depressed. I remember personally feeling defeated like Elijah when I was being pursued and attacked so much of my life. God told Elijah not once but twice to "Get up and eat" to be strengthened for the journey ahead. I love the significance of stopping to rest and be strengthened first before taking on a challenge. Often, I charge into things without first being nourished, not just physically but also spiritually, mentally, and emotionally. When Elijah had traveled 40 days and nights to Horeb and hid in a cave, God asked him, "What are you doing here?" and God ordered him to go out on the mountain and STAND!

"Stand" refers to a position we take of resting in God's power and presence. The wind, earthquake, and fire all came but the Lord was not in it. God told Elijah to "Go back the way you came." God always sends us back until we get it right. And, when we go back, we are to do it differently. The thing with God is He is very patient and not ever in a hurry. Remember that with the Lord a day is like a thousand years, and a thousand years are like a day (2 Peter 3:8). Might it be possible that some of the things we are waiting for God to do are being delayed because He is waiting on us to do what He's called us to? I am learning through stopping these treatments that God is still wanting to heal and deliver me but in a different way now. This time, I have to go back and dig up all the unprocessed trauma and do the work to heal my soul. Anything worthwhile is going to take some level of sacrifice.

I can't get that drawing out of my head. It's been three months now since my EMDR therapist had me do "the drawing" like the ones you see on television where the shrink takes out the white piece of paper and colored markers. She then instructs her client to draw how she feels, and they then discuss the results. I guess this is where the phrase "a picture is worth a thousand words" comes from. I'll be honest in admitting that it seems cliche and childish, yet my results still have me praying about what my drawing means. Why am I lying face up in tall green grass with a big foot centered over my entire chest as if it's about to stomp on me? Talking to my therapist, I shared that it's me lying down and the foot, I think, represents problems from my marriage and illness trying to crush me.

"It's like this HUGE weight of conflict bearing down on me so hard that it's suffocating me, making it hard to breathe," I say. "It's like I'm in the weeds of life but I'm looking up towards heaven for help from God, but I don't know why I'm lying down. Why am I lying down? Why am I not standing?"

"I don't know. That's for you to discern. Notice too, Erin," she replies, "how out of scale the foot is. It's big in comparison to the rest of your body and the other parts of the drawing."

"Yes, I did notice that right away," I answered. "Hmmm. This is interesting and tells me a lot without really telling me anything yet. I'm going to be praying about it and see what the Holy Spirit reveals."

That session ended as the previous ones did after 45 minutes, and my ride home was silenced from all outside noises and distractions as I talked to God about why I was lying down in that drawing. Perplexed and frustrated with myself, I couldn't get this image out of my mind and the disappointment and disgust I felt seeing myself down on the ground and not standing. Why when

I feel like I've been fighting non-stop am I lying down? I don't watch a lot of television, but I've seen enough therapy scenes in various shows over the years to decipher hidden clues to current problems in these types of drawings. And, lying down in tall grass doesn't seem to be a positive thing. Am I crazy? Has all this stress finally gotten to me, and I'm now taking it all lying down? What is happening?

That drawing! I wonder where I put that drawing of me in the grass? Sitting down in my big blue poofy quiet time chair, I take out my Bible and begin to read and pray. I love these times so much that some days I don't want to leave this spot. Dwelling in His presence is growing me and healing me. It's not a religious practice that I do to check any boxes but instead a heart's desire of mine to get to know my Heavenly Father more intimately. The Bible is His love letter to us and has every solution to every problem. I now absolutely adore reading and lingering in His Word. I asked the Holy Spirit to come upon me and fill me with a fresh fire for the Word and its understanding and those prayers were answered. The Bible is a spiritual book written by a spiritual being. We think too much in terms of our physical being when we are 99% spirit. Therefore, we are spirits having a human experience and NOT the other way around. This is the way we need to approach God's Word and life in general. Let the Bible read us instead of us reading the Bible.

God distinctly told me last year when I stopped all my treatments that He was calling me into studying His Word. I got the sense that it wasn't just reading the Bible but, instead, being a diligent student of it—reading, meditating, and praying over scripture. And, now that my life has slowed down, I am learning what it means to be fruitful as opposed to busy.

In Genesis Chapter 12, the Lord calls out Abraham to leave his country and family and go to the land that He would show him. No details were given. He was going into the unknown. Abraham obeyed. Power is when we live in agreement with God. We don't have to understand the "why." We merely are called to obey. I felt like Abraham last May when God said to stop everything that I knew, trust Him, and begin studying. He clearly told me that His Word would heal me, so I am advancing down that path of obedience. It's been really challenging not to fill my life up with other commitments.

My emotions are shattering. The decades of stress are cumbersome, and there's so much to sort through. I believe most people wouldn't want to take the time or effort to get to the root of emotional trauma also as I have with the physical. But I want to do it right, and I'm committed to doing it God's way even though it's painstakingly difficult. It requires rolling up my sleeves, spending a lot of time warring in prayer, and facing things about myself that aren't very pretty.

The Christian is called to be a soldier in God's army. While doing EMDR, Monica told me that "your family is going to hate this!" I didn't understand for a while what she meant until I began digging deeper into my healing journey to get to the root causes of some of this illness. I am totally convinced that psychology and physiology are interrelated. Dealing with all this back pain must also have some ties to emotions, and I'm set on learning everything I can to heal it from the inside out. The inner man is key. We are intricate beings with all systems interwoven. Sometimes, we must go back to move forward. I'm beginning to understand now what Monica was talking about. Digging stuff up from the past and taking it from the darkness to the light is messy. And it's painful. God's domain is the light while Satan's is darkness so anything needing healing needs to be brought out into the light. Luke and I are arguing a lot, and it feels like spiritual warfare is at an all-time high for me. I want to quit so many times each week, but I can't. This life verse plays over and over and over in my mind:

> "Do not grow weary in doing good for in due time, you will reap a harvest IF you DO NOT GIVE UP" (Galatians 6:9).

> *Do NOT give up! Do NOT give up! Stay in your race! The MIRACLE IS COMING! Never EVER give up!*

God is interested in healing our entire being–spirit, soul, and body. I realized as I began healing my brain that the mind and the brain are two different things. The Bible doesn't talk much about the brain, but it does talk about the mind. After completing six months of my brain rewiring program and EMDR therapy, I stopped those programs and began doing a deep dive into all things related to the mind. First, I started with long hours on my bicycle listening to You Tube tapings of a medical doctor from South Africa who teaches the Bible from a healing perspective.

My interest piqued right away and started the new chapter of investigating my new road forward. I believe God placed me in this slower life season now to make this my number one priority. Sometimes, we all need a "pause" season. With the kids all grown up, two moved out of the house and the youngest finishing up high school, now is the time for me to do this work. Surrounding myself with scripture cards, handwritten index cards with verses on them, I find myself living daily with a fresh new ferocious hunger for the Word of God to read, learn and study. This clearly is from the Holy Spirit! This is the first time I've ever felt this dialed in. I can't get enough! It's like a person who hasn't eaten for a while and is ravenous for food. My physical healing hinges on getting it right with my soul. I don't get into my car without having one of my favorite Bible teachers on. I don't trust myself without Jesus. I need the Holy Spirit like I never knew I did before. I am like a deep pit, and I need to be filled with anything and everything related to Him. My soul craves learning like my body craves dark chocolate. I sought out the Transformational Prayer Ministry (TPM) at my church and worked with my pastor's wife and daughter in learning how to transform at the mind/heart level. Recently, I completed my last session and moved between different modalities at God's leading. Weekend getaways are planned as I bring different devotional study guides and books to help sort through all the junk! Amidst the shattering, I'm able to see the dust that now the Potter can use to rework and remake me.

Opening my journal, I see a white piece of paper folded in half. As I open it, I realize it's the drawing that's been haunting me for months. Finally! Here it is. I still don't have the answers I believe are right after dozens of times asking for clarity. So, I ask one more time. It's not enough to solely cry out to God in the secret place but also to look for opportunities to see Him displayed.

"Holy Spirit, please show me what this means! Give me wisdom and discernment. I need eyes to see and ears to hear. Why am I lying down, and why is this huge foot bearing down on me?"

As I sit quietly in my chair with my smallest dog at my side, I instantly hear the Lord speak to me the truth of what this drawing represents. My mouth gasps open and tears start their cascading flow.

How can I be so stupid, I say aloud multiple times. Oh my gosh. That foot isn't my husband or Lyme or any other of these illnesses. It's the Enemy. It's Satan. It's the Devil. He's alive and well on planet earth, and he fooled me all this time. I'm lying down because it's showing that I haven't been walking in the authority and power that Jesus died to give me. God calls us to STAND. I have been deceived in my thinking! And the foot is over my chest because that's where my heart is, and it needs some work.

"Hope deferred makes the heart sick but a longing fulfilled is a tree of life" (Proverbs 13:12).

Frozen in time, too many thoughts are racing through my mind at once, and it's all I can do to process them. I feel like I've been sucker punched right in the gut. And then, I feel overjoyed that I can now see the foundational truth. The Enemy brings condemnation, but the Bible says there is no condemnation in Christ. I take a minute to thank the Holy Spirit for bringing this to my attention because now EVERYTHING is about to change for the better. He brings conviction and that's what I feel.

Ignorance is the Devil's playground. Knowledge is power. We have to take responsibility and study the Word. The Enemy wants us to stay locked up in deception and self-pity while God calls us higher and says we are more than a conqueror through Christ Jesus (Romans 8:37). This means we already know our outcome is going to be victorious before we enter the problem. We need to have times where we take "think breaks" and ask ourselves what we are thinking about. When we are depressed or angry, it could be that we have our mind on things contrary to encouragement and joy. Seventy-five to ninety-eight percent of current mental, physical, and behavioral illness comes from our thought life–our brain is influenced by our mind, our body, and our life. Changed thoughts lead to a changed life!

John 10:10 says, "The thief comes only to steal, kill and destroy but Jesus came to give life and in abundance." I feel so stupid. How can I be a Christian walking with the Lord all these decades and not knowing that the Devil is real and wreaking havoc all over this earth and personally in my life? No one in church ever taught me straight out (or maybe they did but I don't recall) that the Devil seeks to destroy us through our thoughts! Bondage is a household of thoughts. All this time, I have been looking at the illnesses and my husband as the enemy and not seeing who the REAL Enemy is. Satan isn't the red costumed character with horns that we see on Halloween. He is alive and well on planet Earth and wants nothing more than to keep us from our destiny.

The spiritual glasses I wore are now replaced with new ones, and suddenly everything is changing. My life seems like a movie script rolling through scene after scene with these new lenses on. Through my running and racing especially, I've experienced Holy Spirit power and yet, I didn't have eyes to see what the big picture was–the Enemy trying to take me out! Satan, the Bible says, is the Father of all lies and the Accuser of the brethren. Oh, my goodness! This changes EVERYTHING! He's been after me all these years trying to take me out, and if God hadn't revealed this all to me now through the Holy Spirit, he might have won. But now I SEE, and now I HEAR and just as my focus word for this year is "free," I feel like that weighted foot doesn't stand a chance as the Bible says, "Now the Lord is the Spirit, and where the Spirit of the Lord is, there is freedom" (2 Corinthians 3:17). Hell will pay.

"And if he be found, he shall restore sevenfold;
he shall give all the substance of his house"
(Proverbs 6:31).

And to think all this time, I thought those therapist office drawings were ridiculous. This one just changed my life for the best.

Chapter 25

Party of Two

◇◇◇◇◇◇◇◇◇◇◇◇◇◇◇◇◇◇◇◇

"Bye, Luke, I'm headed out!" I announce, walking over to give him a hug goodbye for the day. The race site is only about an hour and a half drive, so I'll be back by early afternoon.

"OK, good luck at your race," he answers, getting himself ready to go run with his group. "How are you feeling?"

"Thanks! And OK. I'm not going to win any prize or anything because right now I'm slow from doing that reset, but I need to get back on the trails where I feel alive and back in the game. I'm not expecting much but to just get out and move. I really feel like a totally different person now. It's crazy. And even though I want to compete, for the first time I don't feel the need inside to beat myself up at all costs. I wish you could see the difference in how much I've changed inside. It blows me away!"

"That's great!" he replies. "Have fun."

And with that, I head out on this dark, chilly winter day.

I like to get to the area where I'm running in plenty of time to kick around if I'm early. Then, at least I'm close by and can sit in my car or make that extra pit stop to calm my nerves. There's nothing worse for me than stressing out that I'm going to be late. Today is no different. It's still about three hours until race time, but I always factor the drive along with three pit stops, just in case. I've been doing this for so long that I have the timing down to a science. And I love going alone so I can listen to some favorite

Bible podcasts, talk to God, or listen to my favorite worship music. Luke and I still race separately most of the time because he doesn't do trail running and that's my favorite. Though he's slowing down after going hard for almost 25 years, he's still doing a few triathlons and road races a year.

Running is revealing so much to me as a person. How amazingly fitting that a new decade of life is quickly approaching, and I believe one for which God has been preparing me all my life. I can't recall being truly happy in a while, although joy rooted in Christ has permeated my life. Don't get me wrong, there have been MANY life events, mostly all surrounding my kids and family, that brought me tremendous happiness, excitement, and fulfillment, but I am referring to the overall state of happiness in relation to my physical feelings. There has always been an opposing force between the two and experiencing victory now in my soul is making all this new effort in healing worth it. It sounds crazy, but I'm learning how to be happy because with many of my symptoms now gone, it's like I finally get to exhale a bit. That would make anyone happy. The world would have us believe that life exists in everything physical where we can be so easily brought down by our circumstances instead of continually looking to Jesus, the author and perfecter of our faith. No one ever could have told me how hard it would be if I wanted something so badly for someone else that the burden of concern would interfere with my ability to let go and trust God fully. It seems the deeper I go, the deeper God calls me and the stronger the obstacles become. It's been a challenge to surrender my grip on being fooled into believing I had control in the first place. That's another Enemy's lie. It's not my job to "carry the team," as one counselor pointed out. Discovering soul wounds created in childhood provides vital knowledge in healing today's hurts. The saying goes that hurting people hurt people. We all would benefit by taking time to go back to the lies we created and believed during childhood and replace it with God's truth.

What we create in our minds becomes our reality and learning to walk in new patterns is often daunting, but doable, life-giving, and changing. If there's one driving point here to make, it's that Satan hates us and seeks to keep us out of our God-ordained destiny by means of our mind. It takes 21 days to reconstruct a new thought after deconstructing an old one and 63 days to cement that thought into a habit. Our mind is where we find God's will to understand, but it's not the source of it. We think four to seven thoughts at a time in our conscious mind with four hundred billion actions per second in our unconscious mind. "The mind is starting to understand what the spirit already knows," Dr. Caroline Leaf, an expert in neuroscience says. Additionally, she mentions:

- The brain cannot generate the mind; the brain simply houses the mind
- Worship is designed for the highest part of man
- 98.999% is our non-conscience state (years of thoughts and memories)
- We have 3 MILLION + years of brain storage
- There are 100 billion neurons in our brain
- Every part of our body is impacted with every thought and others around us
- There are 300 scriptures that THOUGHTS precede action

"For God has not given us a spirit of fear but one of LOVE, POWER and a SOUND MIND" (2 Timothy 1:7).

- What we think about drives our body
- Being Born Again (receiving Jesus as our personal Savior by grace through faith) regenerates our spirit and allows us to be plugged into Holy Spirit
- We use existing memories to form current new ones

If our mind determines our reality, then we become what we think! In 2 Corinthians 10:3-5 we learn:

"For though we live in the world, we do NOT wage war as the world does. The weapons we fight with are NOT the weapons of the world. On the contrary, they have divine POWER to demolish strongholds. We demolish arguments and every pretension that sets itself up against the knowledge of God and we take every thought captive to the obedience of Christ."

It sounds so obvious but the obvious wasn't always obvious to me. We can decide to keep thoughts or not as they enter our mind and can "take it captive" (I picture a big crab/fishing net), meaning to grab it or release it. We decide with the filter of God's truth. We come into agreement with what God says and partner with Him. If it's a godly thought, we keep it, and if it's not, we dispose of it. The Bible says to "cast down wrong thoughts" and the word "cast" is a violent action. It means to demolish! It's a weapon of our warfare talked about in Ephesians 6 as we bear the Armor of God. This is the helmet of salvation–right thinking! Let's Armor Up in the full armor every day as we run our race and contend for the faith!

Recalling a recent conversation with my favorite senior, godly counselor, he said to me in his angelically-toned, slow Southern twang, "Erin, stop tryin' (trying) and start dyin' (dying)!" This impactful sentence ruminates in my mind regularly. As Christians, we are called to put off the old nature and put on the new nature of Christ. This requires a lifetime of sanctification. I figure I'll be around at least 100 years still working on this dying and not trying thing. I still have a long way to go but now I can receive grace through faith to live it out one moment at a time and rest in my Creator's goodness and faithfulness. AHHHHHH, does this feel heavenly!

Miracles in my life are happening continually! One of the biggest ones is being antibiotic free for three years and counting. Finally, I experience breakthroughs as I continue pressing into what God promised. I love the parable of the persistent friend in Luke 11. He knocks at his friend's house to get bread, and the friend refuses to wake up and unlock the door. But, because of the boldness of the one knocking, the friend eventually gets up and gives him as much as he needs. Jesus then proceeds to remind us to ASK, SEEK, and KNOCK, and it will be given to us. Notice these are all action words and require continued action. We must KEEP asking, KEEP seeking, and KEEP knocking! Our miracle may be one door opening away. Don't quit now!

Miracles happen in three ways: the supernatural, the natural, and the medical.

First, there is the SUPERNATURAL miraculous healing of God where an encounter happens between Jehovah Rapha, the Mighty Physician, and by the touch of His hand only. There is divine intervention. The illness or situation suddenly is made new again and restoration takes place. God redeems the time in a moment. It's not of our doing or anyone else's. These miracles are less common but absolutely exist today, and I believe they are ramping back up as we come into a time of awakening and revival. I'm expecting to witness more of these firsthand.

The second type of healing is NATURAL. God made our body to heal itself. He knit us together in our mother's womb and designed the perfect immune system to act as our defense. Environmental factors come into play often weakening this system, but it was perfectly designed to fight, repair, and protect. Often, we do our part by eating well, exercising, reducing stress in our life, getting proper sleep, and other healthy activities that the body uses for keeping us up and running.

Additionally, mental, and emotional health are just as vital, if not even more important. For me, getting into the Word of God and declaring His truths over my life and body brings continual healing to it as well as my soul and spirit. The Bible talks a lot about God's words having the power of healing in our life. He spoke the world into existence and keeps it all running by the power of His words. In any instant, God could speak a word to cause it all to fall or to turn it all around for the better. Often, we fail to acknowledge and utilize the POWER He's given us through words. For me, helpful passages include:

> "He sent out his word and healed them; he rescued them from the grave" (Psalm 107:20).

> "But I will restore you to health and heal your wounds, declares the Lord…" (Jeremiah 30:17).

> "Do not be wise in your own eyes; fear the Lord (love what He loves and hate what He hates) and shun evil. This will bring health to your body

and nourishment/refreshment to your bones" (Proverbs 3:7-8).

"My son, pay attention to what I say; listen closely to my words. Do not let them out of your sight, keep them within your heart; for they are life to those who find them and health to a man's whole body. Above all else, guard your heart for it is the wellspring of life" (Proverbs 4:20–23).

"Guard my teachings as the apple of your eye" (Proverbs 7:2).

"Reckless words pierce like a sword, but the tongue of the wise brings healing" (Proverbs 12:18).

"A heart at peace gives life to the body, but envy rots the bones" (Proverbs 15:30).

"The tongue that brings healing is a tree of life, but a deceitful tongue crushes the spirit" (Proverbs 15:4).

"Pleasant words are a honeycomb, sweet to the soul and healing to the bones" (Proverbs 16:24).

"A cheerful heart is good medicine, but a crushed spirit dries up the bones" (Proverbs 17:22).

"The tongue has the power of life and death, and those who love it will eat its fruit" (Proverbs 18:21).

In the Bible, James describes the tongue as a fire that can corrupt the entire person and that no man can tame because of its restless evil and fullness of poison (James 3). A life can change when the words one speaks change. This is healing me, my marriage, and other relationships as I learn and apply these principles. This is challenging for me because words are my love language and it's like a double-edged sword. As much as great encouraging words exit my mouth to build others up, so are words that criticize and tear down. God is dealing with me a lot in this area. I'm learning especially in my marriage how damaging my words have been as well as ones I speak over me. The Enemy wants us to believe the worst about others while God helps us see the best. My prayer each day is to see others through His eyes. Some days, that's a lot easier than others.

Lastly, the third type of healing is MEDICAL. For me, most of my past healing came from this avenue. God opened the doors to competent, anointed men and women who were instruments in my healing! God uses people to carry out His work, and I wouldn't be here today if not for these amazing doctors who partnered with me. I call them the miracles in motion and this type of healing can take a very long time as mine has. Never give up hope that God is going to redeem each painful symptom or circumstance. He is willing. He is able. He is good. And He is faithful–ALL the time! I think this is where many of us stop short of our miracle–giving up too soon! Can I please encourage you, friend, to stay in your race AS LONG AS IT TAKES for the miracle to manifest! So far, with all the work I've partnered with God in, many of my infections, ailments, and symptoms have disappeared and/or are improving. It's been a fight, but the harvest is coming! Activated faith requires radical action of determination.

Chapter 26

Let Go and Let God

◇◇◇◇◇◇◇◇◇◇◇◇◇◇◇◇◇◇◇◇◇◇◇◇◇◇◇◇◇◇◇◇◇◇◇◇◇◇

As I pull into the semi-crowded gravel lot, I see runners walking to and from the registration tent, pinning on race bibs, talking, laughing, and carrying the beloved race bags full of useless goodies. I still feel alive as my feet hit the scene, and I hope this lingers throughout the rest of my life. I want to finish strong. Starting and Finishing bookend the real race that happens in the middle. It's the refining process that births the diamond. The promotion results from the promise and the process. If we can keep running our race, refusing to quit, we will look back one day and say it was hard but so worth it. I'm almost ready to say those words…. almost!

I feel giddy and keep smiling at thoughts of how far I've come. It's OK that no one knows the reason behind my smile today. At times throughout my journey, the flame dimmed almost to burning out, but with continual renewed strength, it's reignited brighter than ever before. I feel like I have already won, although the gun has yet to sound.

With my race packet in hand, I sit alone with my thoughts before warming up for the 10k that awaits. February can still be very cold in the South and today is one of those 40-degree days, which for me is perfect running weather. Though I've aged a few years since last competing at these trails at the US National Whitewater Center outside of Charlotte, North Carolina, overall, my outward appearance is the same. However, no one would know how much my inner self has changed since last time racing this course, but I know. And God knows. Today, it's a party for two!

The start is now 30 minutes until "Go time," so I exit the warm car, removing all my toasty clothes in exchange for the shorts and short-sleeved shirt I chose for today. I'm running in my favorite red top given to me at a past race called the Superhero Run. I ran with pictures of my kids on my cape and truly did feel a different type of supernatural power. A cape will do that for you! The flying superhero emblem fills the upper side of my dry wicking shirt and reminds me that I am insufficient in Christ's sufficiency.

Making my way to the first couple of rows, I know I don't have the fitness to go all out with a bang. Though I desire that to be different, I'm OK with where I am. It's about excellence at that moment. Today's excellence may look different than tomorrow's. I may not be running my eight-minute-miles now while I'm learning to let go of the performance perfectionism. For those not athletically wired, it's hard to understand why anyone would push themselves as hard as I have, and others like me. It's hard to put into words, really, but maybe it's best to say our natural bent towards over-achieving results from our past. I still expect a lot out of myself, especially in relation to my natural limitations, but I love to focus on what God of the impossible can do as He calls me to these events.

There are probably close to 300 runners here today, and it's important to get my position on the road before entering the woods. There, the trails narrow to single track formation, so even though I don't have explosive power today, I can at least gain ground merely by being up front.

The gun sounds, and we are off! My breathing labors quickly just as it did last week when God called me back to racing after a seven-month hiatus. I still was running "for fun" during this time but wasn't able to race due to nagging physical injuries and continuing health challenges. I felt very run down after finishing my sixth Run For God session last year and needed to retrain my body to work more efficiently at a lower heart rate. I followed a great program from a well-known runner coach who teaches the proper way to do a HR (heart rate) reset including the formula calculation and steps to being successful. I committed six months to the reset, though the recommended time was three to six months. With my health history, I figured I needed longer, and I faithfully went after it. I thought I was doing the reset for physical reasons only until, one day, I recall deeper ways God spoke to me. The number of heart rate beats for me needed to stay around 125, not under and not over. The theory in physiology is about burning fuel more effectively while keeping the heart in a steadier state of rest without having to work as hard. So, it is with God. He has a rhythm for each one of us that is uniquely ours.

I thought about how I let circumstances, people or events dictate at times my rhythm instead of the other way around. God wants us to find that "sweet spot," that place where we perfectly align with Him. We need to stay in step with HIS rhythm. As we each have a different target heart rate number to follow, so we uniquely fall into different places in our life race with God. My exercise watch flashed "easy" for the zone I worked in but mentally it challenged me to go this slowly. It's a discipline like doing speed work. When my heart rate jumped too high or too low outside that perfect 125 zone, the watch would beep as if to say, "speed up or slow down and come back to this sweet spot." I had to stay in this target zone to get the physical effects desired of being able to push my body harder with less effort. Isn't this how God works as well? If we find Him in our designated "zone" we can be more efficient doing less works of the flesh and resting more in His strength and power by trusting Him.

To measure heart rate improvements, one-mile testing occurred every four weeks at the same track. It was the constant. It was the steady stability of the experiment just like the character of Jesus. As the running reset required discipline, time, and patience, and the testing determined progress or lack thereof, so it is in our life's race. God is patient. The question lies in being able to be patient and loving with ourselves right where we are. If we're going, we're growing, and that's the heart of Jesus. Don't park at the place of pain.

I walked a lot during that 50 participant Viking trail 5k in North Carolina and don't mind if I need to walk some today too. I ended up winning my age group last week due to low turnout and my will to push through the pain and arrive at the Finish Line with a decent time. Of course, I also had a wink from God saying, thanks for obeying and showing up!

The trails here today are muddy and slippery from recent melting snow, and it's adding to my overall zeal! I remember other races here and on other favorite trails where I battled chronic sinus infections taking antibiotics making me sick with all kinds of side effects. My head and face would throb, ears burn, head spin, muscles weaken, cramp and tighten, and joints ache to where all I wanted to do was cry, which I certainly did soon after the race. The race bib reminded me to endure. It whispered to my soul, "God is not done with you yet because you are still alive and moving." Today, the whisper is the same but the body shouts new victory. My body isn't carrying the weight of the past pains. Allergies are nearly gone; muscles are returning to a semi-normal state; no potent medications or natural remedies fill my gut; and, most importantly, my mind feels free! I'm tired, out of shape, and still dealing with musculoskeletal problems as well as some lingering pains that may or may not ever go away. But I'm believing they will and continue pressing on until the breakthrough comes. I'm declaring God's promises over what my circumstances reveal.

Rounding the last corner of the woods before exiting the trails and making our way to the finish via the paved road, my mind fills with the recent heart rate reset God had me do. And it's the reason I am OK today with running more slowly and simply getting out here to run with fellow athletes.

Turning my stride over faster and faster to reach the finish, I charge the final hill with every bit of energy left. I made the entire 6.2 miles without walking. I exceeded my goals for today because my expectations were reasonable. Learning throughout this journey that disappointments are sin, I'm finding contentment now in having mourned what I believed I lost or would never gain again. It's like a death that we must confront and process to attain full healing in our spirit, soul, and body. Working through the disappointments with the Holy Spirit's leading and allowing time to grieve shows us God's mercy and amazing grace. Today is my season to rejoice!

Cooling down by quickly running to the car to gather my warm clothes and coat, I stay around for other runners to finish and for the awards. I'm spent but recharged, exhausted but re-energized, and broken but not crushed. Grabbing water and a snack, I replace some nutrients lost and sit by the warm enclosed firepit by the food tent until the director begins the awards. Names are read for the top three fastest finishers in Age Group categories. Finally, "Women Age Group 45-49…." (Not much longer for me in this group) is announced.

He proceeds to read the names of the third place and second place winners and quickly I realize my time is the fastest of all three. "And the first-place winner goes to Erin Leopold!" he announces.

Shocked but excited, I take my place on the podium block and ask another runner's family member to snap a picture on my phone. After graciously receiving a gift card to a local sports store, I make my way back to my car, smiling from ear to ear! Immediately, I think about the verse in Psalm 27:13 saying, "Surely I will see the goodness of the Lord in the land of the living!" Oh, how true that promise is.

Dialing Luke, the phone rings several times before he picks up. "Hey, how did it go?"

"I actually won my age group believe it or not!" I laughingly say. "I ran the whole way and ran a lot slower than I'm used to, but I guess it was enough for today. To be honest, I'm proud of myself. The course was super muddy and hard and there were a lot of people. It's weird because of all the times I raced out here over the years, this time felt different."

"How did you feel?"

"My body still has a lot of structural and neuropathic pain but so many of my past problems are gone! I'm focusing on all the victories today because I am so thankful! God is worthy to be praised. And He blessed me with a gift card to use at this place's outdoor store," I say.

"That's great! I'm happy for you! Are you coming home soon?" Luke asks.

"Yeah, in a bit. I'm going to go see what this gift amount can buy then make my way back. I'll see you soon."

Buckling up to head back home, my eyes catch the time, and it's significant. I chuckle and smile and say aloud alone in my car, *of course it is!* The time reads 12:12! Twelve was my jersey number all throughout my days of playing sports and continues to be the favorite number I choose for many situations. Nothing happens by chance or coincidence. God stamped me with that number early on, and I have since received insight from the Holy Spirit leading me to the understanding of this powerful way that God communicates to me through numbers. Twelve marks when God is in control of something and we should remember that anytime we try to help God be God, we will end up in big trouble.

It's almost as if God knew all along that "letting go and letting God" was going to be a lifetime of learning for me and the exact area in my life that screamed of needed pruning. He's great like that. OK, yes, I'm way too much of a control freak but, thankfully, it's not a surprise to God. He loves me just the same. And, today, I already knew in my soul the victories I won, yet He once again stretched out His hand to mine and said, "Don't worry. I've got you. Let go and trust Me!"

Open hands meet outstretched arms. Grab on today!

Chapter 27

Over The Finish Line

◇◇

It's 4:00 am and never have I been this excited to be awake at this hour. I'd like to say I slept a solid eight hours but that would be a far stretch from the three to four I got and not in consecutive order. But it's OK. Sleep is overrated anyway and, sadly, for the past six plus years, I've been up and down a handful of times and not getting the deep restorative sleep like I used to. I know how important quality sleep is to health, so it's my constant quest, especially now that menopause is in full swing, and all kinds of hormonal craziness exists. If it's not one thing, it's another. Whoever said God gives us what we can handle clearly misspoke. He *does* certainly give us more than we can handle so that we will turn to Him in and for all things.

Gathering up the last items for my suitcase, and, yes, it's still pushing the 50-pound weight limit, I run down the list of essentials then tether the last strap and zip it up. Arriving at the airport, Luke and I get our bags checked in quickly, head through security, and await our boarding. We decided just the two of us would take this quick four-day trip so our youngest wouldn't miss any schooling and be able to care for the pups.

Anxiously awaiting to board the plane, I steady my thoughts and nerves by talking to God.

I wouldn't be here today without Him. It's been at least eight years since I last flew out West so today is a HUGE test for me. These past several years of healing my soul were not without hardships and newly discovered challenges. But, taking time to heal the buried live emotions through processing God's truth is bringing me continued health and restoration. These past wounds are closing and not carrying the same emotional charge they once did. I want to be done with bleeding into my present life from past wounds. Even though I'm petrified to get on this flight because past trips brought so much bodily pain and mental angst, I have a peace today knowing that won't happen anymore because I'm healed!

"Are you excited for the concert?" Luke asks.

"I CANNOT wait!" I answer. "I know you like her music too, but I wish I could explain to you how meaningful and impactful her lyrics are that literally kept me moving forward in hope. Her music literally was my rescue repeatedly. I ran so many runs singing those words as battle cries in my head with tears streaming down my face. It's not like I'm just excited to go see another artist sing songs that I like. This is all about a huge test, a final stamp, an 'I made it' victory dance, if you will. I don't feel like the same person inside that I was. Even though I still have a lot of lingering physical symptoms, I believe I am healed. It's all so hard to explain, to be honest."

"That's good!" he proclaims. "I'm happy for you, and I hope it continues."

"Luke, I know we've been through a lot; I mean a lot. I apologize for all the ways that I've hurt you and ask for your forgiveness. I'm committed to my total healing and doing my part in our marriage and for our family. I want to thank you again for surprising me with these tickets and this trip. I know though you don't understand much of this, you at least know how much this concert and time out West means to me right now. I appreciate it and am more grateful than you'll ever know. It's one of the best gifts I've ever received. Thank you," I add.

"Flight 2417 to Denver, Colorado now boarding all remaining passengers," the attendant announces.

Luke and I grab our carry-ons and enter the plane. Thankfully, it's a two-seater row so I get my favorite seat by the window and don't feel apologetic for having to get up multiple times during the flight to use the restroom. Water is still my drink of choice, and it's with me all throughout the day, every day. The air on the plane always gives me a bad headache so I drink extra to combat some of the dehydration from elevation changes.

The three-and-a-half-hour direct flight goes smoothly with only a few bumpy patches, and I now have some new history of success to replace the old with. It feels like Christmas morning as a child and Santa delivered the greatest gift I asked for. I said for a long time that my rebirth was coming at age 50, and it's here. God says, "See and taste that the Lord is good" (Psalm 34:8). He absolutely is. Once I realized I ingested the Devils' lies that I'd be dead by age 50, I chose to believe the Voice of Truth instead, and here I am finally thriving instead of merely surviving. Proverbs 18:21 says "the power of life and death are in the tongue." I have to continue speaking LIFE! God isn't only interested in our thoughts but the process of how we think. I believe it and feel it in every part of my being. No matter what ailments still inhabit me, I can now see and remember the breakthroughs I had in so many areas: NO antibiotics for a handful of years, gut healing from the many protocols enabling me to eat and enjoy a wider spectrum of foods, significantly fewer female infections, regular migraines completely gone, chronic headaches very rare, allergies like "normal" people with seasonal sniffles but able to go outdoors and actually enjoy it; muscles and joints feeling more normal and stronger; daily energy, steady and solid; dizziness nearly gone although flaring up only on minimal occasions, and, overall, a mind that looks at every situation in a brand new light and appreciates the smallest of things that many miss. I look back often to answered prayer, pointing directly to the faithfulness of God.

"OK," Luke announces as the plane lands, and we enter our gate. "We made it!"

"Yep!" I answer. "Thank goodness it's only one flight. That helps a lot. This was great. The vibration of the plane still ignites my nervous system and I have a headache and some nausea but, overall, much better than ever before!" I feel like I just won the lottery and passed that darn test. Mountains are my happy place! It feels so good to be back in Colorado and, so far, I'm not having any of my past elevation problems. I have landed multiple times in the emergency room here skiing in years prior, so this is a wonderful experience getting to finally enjoy all the sights and sounds of what I love most–God's glorious outdoor playground. No more going around some of those "mountains" I went around for years. This is the new Erin.

Luke says, "I'm glad you feel better."

Luke continues to be a man of fewer words, but I'm learning how important it is to let him off the potter's wheel and allow the true potter, God, to mold, shape, and grow him as He desires. I'll admit, I did a lot wrong in the marriage department and the standout takeaway is in owning my share of the responsibility. I gave up my story. We become so attached to that script that we go through mourning and loss, trying to leave the familiar. The past several years, I fought to exit the known wilderness area. I desired and ran after knowledge to cover myself in new wineskin, so I'd be ready for the new "wine" God seeks to pour into our lives. I want it for my health but also my marriage and family. We all went through a lot, and I continue learning that I am only responsible for myself. But, with my zealous personality to "fix it," I spent too much time focused on the other person instead of staying in my lane and taking my concerns, fears, and brokenness to God.

I remember one day in the car driving with Luke and a huge fight broke out. I continued running my mouth with all sorts of advice, criticism, and scripture he needed to apply. If God speaks to us through the Holy Spirit in ways we understand, then I received the biggest finger "thump" on the temple of my forehead with these words: "Would you just be quiet and let Me work!"

"The Lord will fight for you if you remain calm and keep silent" (Exodus 14:14). Holy smokes is this difficult for me! Thank goodness we have the Holy Spirit to help us and a lifetime of mercy and grace.

Finally, it's time to drive to the Red Rocks Amphitheater for the concert, and I still can't believe I get to see Lauren Daigle. People come from all over the world to see artists perform at Red Rocks because of its spectacular beauty. To think Luke surprised me with tickets and a small getaway because he knew how instrumental she was and is in my healing makes me very happy. He's not one to surprise me with things like this, so it's huge. A marked moment for sure! I feel heard. I feel believed in. And I feel really loved. It's all been worth it! There, I said it. I wouldn't want to do it all again, yet I am thankful for the gift disguised as the curse. This is what I signed up for.

Looking back a moment to see how I got here today with Luke, I hearken back to something powerfully spoken in my soul when he was having a recent outpatient procedure done. It was a pivotal moment for me, and a difficult one. It brings me healing now and the continual movement forward in my marriage. Trauma is real, and, boy, did I suffer with it. I didn't realize all the emotions I suppressed over the years and how often I went to bed angry. And the power of my words! God says anger is acceptable. He gets angry. But it's sinning while angry that causes the problem. It's here that it becomes ground for the Enemy to take and, if we aren't careful, over time, harboring anger builds to a stronghold where the Enemy camps out, hides, and wreaks havoc in our life. The Bible aptly says in Ephesians 5 not to go to bed angry "as to give the devil a foothold." One or two nights isn't the problem but it's the continuation of doing this night after night, week after week, year after year. Then, a stronghold sets up in our mind and heart.

God, through His mercy and grace, began showing me areas in my life that couldn't heal because of unresolved anger, bitterness, and unforgiveness. I had a deep root of bitterness that was producing this bad fruit. That bitterness traced back to a wrong belief that God was holding out when He could have intervened and changed things. I believe this is at the foundation of many Christians' pain. I thought because He is Sovereign, the Ruler and Creator of the Universe, that He should've healed many of the situations I faced. I didn't understand how spiritual laws operate. I now understand that because He IS Sovereign, it would go against His character to step in continually because He did not create us to be robots. He gave us free will, and we live in a fallen sinful world of illness and pain. Thus, bad things sometimes happen to good people.

Healing begins with sanctification of the heart. I cannot think of anything more powerful to change the course of our life than this: HEALING UNFORGIVENESS IS ABSOLUTELY ESSENTIAL FOR HEALING AND FOR LIFE SUCCESS.

God tells us in Matthew 6:14-15, "For if you forgive men when they sin against you, your heavenly Father will also forgive you. BUT, if you do not forgive men their sins, your father will not forgive your sins." Also, in Matthew 18, Jesus says, "This is how my heavenly Father will treat each of you unless you forgive your brother from your heart." There's that forgiveness in the heart part again. I know I have read these verses countless times, yet it took until now to really get my attention in such a way as to put it into practice! Now, every night I ask God to do a heart check in me and anything left unattended I take before the Lord and ask for forgiveness. It's like a daily reset. I can't afford to carry any of this around in me any longer. My words created encouragement, hope, and life for so many, yet they also tore down areas in my own health and marriage. Words go out like missiles on a mission, and if I want positive turnarounds, then it's my job to speak what I desire.

James 4:2 says, "You receive not because you ask not." Instead of praying against what we don't want, we need to tell God what we DO want.

Mark 11:25 states, "If you hold anything against anyone, forgive him, so that your Father in heaven may forgive you your sins." Wow! There it is again.

"Unforgiveness and forgiveness may be the most critical issues in anyone's life," Dr. Alex Loyd, the founder of the Healing Codes says. After talking to ministers, doctors, therapists, and practitioners of all kinds, his consensus is that unforgiveness is at the root of just about every problem they've experienced. Dr. Loyd states that "unforgiveness often hides behind anger, fear, sadness, and other things like that. Unforgiveness issues can be towards self, other people, and even God."

The word "forgiveness" in its original Greek language means to "cut or untie the rope." Even if the person isn't willing to accept our apology and forgive us, forgiveness frees us from the bondage.

Forgiveness is about us. It allows our hearts to be free and give God a place to work. I believe this is one of the biggest things I did for my total healing and continue doing today. Maintenance is a present goal!

Forgiveness, reconciliation, and trust are all different things. We can forgive someone but not trust them nor desire reconciliation. That's perfectly OK depending on the relationship and situation. Forgiveness often comes in levels of degree. We can't let the Enemy talk us out of our forgiveness. God says once we repent, He remembers it no more! It's done. It's erased as far as the East is from the West. Though I've done a huge amount of forgiving for areas I felt neglected and hurt by, it's still an ongoing process including to reconcile and trust. It isn't easy but God never said it would be, but that faith would make it possible.

The Holy Spirit also brought to my attention, after years of work in this area of healing, many specific examples of being angry at myself and at God. It's crazy to think now how I could ever be angry at God, but I was. Someone may be in a similar place today. Can I please urge you to take time alone and sit with the Holy Spirit and ask Him to show your areas that need forgiveness and healing? Inaction is also an action. I had lost sight that the Enemy has reign over the earth and its fallen nature and it's God who we need to keep as our best Friend and steady Helper.

Fear is another huge trap of the Enemy! It's a spirit not given to us by God. Fear can come in the form of anger, depression, sadness, manipulation, and dishonesty. There is fear of failure as well as fear of success. It's normal to feel fear and, when we do, take it to God to align our thoughts and actions with His Word. This is life-changing and life-giving! The recipe for living the abundant life Jesus died to give us. I'm going after it!

The air fills with a nice breeze keeping the evening temperature to around 75 degrees. I couldn't ask for a more perfect night. Sitting, standing, praising hands in the air, belting out all the rescue lyrics I cried my way through during this excruciating journey, my heart feels peaceful. The Denver skyline lights the backdrop of the stage, and it's glorious. Surrounded by huge rock boulders and a landscape too beautiful to put into words and one only appreciated by experiencing it, I can't think of anywhere else I'd rather be or with anyone else but the man who stood by me throughout the darkest season of my life. He's nowhere near perfect nor am I, yet we commit to choosing to love every day of our lives. Love is not an emotion but rather a decision. Yeah, I wish a lot could've been different but isn't that how it is with every relationship in life? It's all in our attitude and how we see the cup. Do we see it half full or half empty? God is regularly teaching me in marriage and life to shine light on the good and not the bad. A thankful heart goes a long way!

The concert adjourns, and my heart overflows with emotion. Every song I hold dear. Although Lauren and I never met, it seems that we are best friends or at least soul sisters. Her lyrics transcend demographics and circumstances. Now all I can think about is getting back here first thing in the morning to run up these amphitheater stairs at sunrise. I may not be able to sleep tonight awaiting this dream!

"Did you like the concert?" Luke asks.

"Did I like it? Oh my gosh, it was AMAZING! I literally cannot put into words how great it was and the impact this is having on me. But now I got to go to bed so I can get up and run!" I answer.

"You're still getting up early to run the amphitheater?"

"Heck yeah! That's one of the things I've looked forward to most. After you and the boys sent pictures last year on your visit here of people working out at sunrise, I have been dreaming of it. Are you going to come?" I question.

"What time again are you getting up?"

"Like 5:00 am. I want to be there in plenty of time to be parked and running before the sun makes its entrance," I answer.

"Would you be mad if I didn't go? I don't want to get up that early. It's like 11:30 pm now, and I need some sleep," he says.

A bit miffed but also excited to have this time alone, I respond, "That's fine. It's your loss. I'm going!"

"Look Up Child" plays on my phone signaling the 5:00 am wakeup call! I got only a few hours of sleep anticipating what's in front of me. It's not about the running. Yes, I still do like the health benefits, but continued suffering from the musculoskeletal problems and lingering Lyme related issues make it a continual challenge physically. But I don't care. I don't live based on my feelings.

Arriving at the parking lot, I see very few cars here but enough that I don't feel alone. With air pods, water, and a gym bag full of other running essentials, I climb the multi flights of stairs to enter the amphitheater. The air is cool and perfect for running. The darkness begins to lighten as the sun prepares to make its grand debut. I make my way down to the bottom of the arena, ready to take on the 50 rows and four miles of running back and forth through each. There are probably 10 other athletes here doing various workouts with a couple running as well and a few people sitting in the stillness of the morning. It's heavenly. I can't stop smiling. It doesn't matter that at 6800 feet above sea level that I'm losing my breath upon starting and having to push extra hard to keep myself going. I'm a warrior and a champion, not by the world's standards, but by God's.

No age group win is coming my way today, and that's the way I want it to be. This is my own race of sorts. It's my life's race and only God and I know the details of the course. Some days, the mountains were too steep to climb, but I overcame them because my heart believed I would when my mind said otherwise. Some days, the wind blew fiercely in my face and still my feet carried me to new places of breakthrough and discovery. All the early mornings rushing out the door to meet the sun (Son) and receive the new day's mercies landed me here. My Coach prepared the way long before my feet knew the miles needed to carry me across the Finish Line. He always answered my calls. He always gave perfect advice. He always cheered me on when I so desperately wanted to quit and helped me find my second wind when weakness crippled my body and soul. He is my Rock. He is my Anchor. He is the God of the Universe who reaches down into my world to call me to His own because of His love for me. He chooses ordinary people like me to call the apple of His eye.

Reaching the final top row and hearing my Garmin display four miles, the sun breaks through the clouds, and my heart rejoices at the celebration of life! I pause to thank Yeshewa, Abba Father, Jehovah Jireh, and Jehovah Rapha for getting me here today to the top of the mountain where I stand looking down at the place where I began. My breathing is labored and my muscles strain, but my soul releases a new energy shouting, "New beginnings are here and yours for the taking!" The race hasn't been easy, but it's been worth it!

The flight home goes without incident, and we settle back into our daily routine. I'm still on my Rocky Mountain High, which I'm hoping will carry me through for a very long time. This will forever be one of my greatest life blessings! I'm not used to feeling this much peace amidst trying times, but I'm loving it and ready to keep it going. While searching for a particular book in my nightstand drawer, I find myself clearing out all the old unneeded stuff. As I search, I find a couple of old letters and journal entries I wrote during the toughest years of my battle against chronic illness and disease. The words are sharp and piercing, but something is different now. These few letters all contain memories that once shattered my soul, times of darkness that I wanted to run away from and give up on and times when others very close to me shamed and judged me harshly. The pain cut deeply. As I read the words now sentence by sentence, I realize something very unusual and different within me. It doesn't burn. It doesn't sting. Although I'm saddened by what it says, I'm not affected any longer by an angry response or deep woundedness in my soul. The words are simply letters filling a page because my thoughts no longer grant them power. This is a breakthrough and a huge win! I believe this may be what transformation is all about!

Quietly sitting alone on the edge of my bed, I decide I no longer need any of these reminders of the pain that once tried to take me out. The Devil has no legal right to me because I belong to God. I know now what having that resurrection power and authority He has given to us looks like and how to walk in it. This time with tears of joy and triumph cascading down my cheeks, I tear the papers to shreds and allow the past to be the past. I finally passed this test.

As I locate the book lining the very bottom of the drawer, my eyes quickly spot three things: a small white feather, a pink construction paper heart cut-out, and a yellow sticky note with the word "You" on it. Years ago, when my kids were younger, I cut out paper hearts to put in their rooms on Valentine's Day with special messages of love on yellow sticky notes. I hadn't done this in a decade or two, yet somehow these remained in the drawer. I have no idea where the feather came from except feathers always seem to show up in the most unexpected places and ways. It's God's reminder to me that He has me covered in the shadow of His wings (Psalm 91:4) and that His angels have been given charge over me (Psalm 91:11). Today, I notice the feather is white as if to represent angel wings and noticing how the three things are placed as if to tell a story, I suddenly hear in my spirit these words:

> *"Erin, I love you. You have been hidden under My wings for all these years where Satan could not touch or harm you. You have been protected in the secret place. My angels have surrounded you from the very moment you believed and received Me as your Personal Savior as a young girl. I promised I would always love you and protect you, and I have done as I said I would do. I am faithful. I never wanted a fight and was always after your heart. I am FOR you and have wanted My very best plan for your life. You have never been alone, and our times of wrestling came because I desired your dreams to align with Mine so I could fulfill and bless them. I needed you to learn how to battle for what My Son's death atoned for and fight not for victory but FROM victory! The work was already done. I've been with you every step of the way. I love you, and I'm proud of you."*

Taking this all in, I settle back onto my soft pillow and allow my mind to replay the clips of empty spaces where I once felt fearful, helpless, bitter, and full of strife. One by one, each painful memory surfaces. I sit with the pain of my past and fill the defeats with victories as I see Jesus in every moving step throughout each extended mile. Peace was always available within me and all I needed to do was release it. How does something that sounds so simple seem so hard?

Tears stain my flushed cheeks recalling the thousands of them shed by a broken soul chasing down courage at every sharp turn. Jesus was always there in the relentless battle waging between my flesh and spirit mind. He was vying for ultimate victory by coming against Enemy lies with God's promised truth. The countless cries for help, the desperate yearnings for brighter days, and the darkest nights that screamed to my worn and shattered soul, "you're not going to make it" were all under God's wings. My part was to stay under that covering, rest, and simply trust Him. I did make it, and His grace was sufficient indeed.

The open Heavens engulf my spirit, soul, and body as a new fresh wind of redemption and restoration blows forth, the transforming life of the lion and the lamb. What the Enemy meant for harm God is using for good. I now know the keys to unlocking the power and authority I have in Christ and how to walk in victory! I press on to run in such a way as to get the prize by finishing this life race strong. My body was never something God intended for me to fix but, instead, a miracle that needed discovering from the One True Source from Whom all power flows.

Afterword

◇◇◇◇◇◇◇◇◇◇◇◇◇◇◇◇◇◇◇

First, I need to acknowledge that the only way I had access to God's promises was because I am His child. God laid upon my heart a large burden to pray for those who walk a similar road of invisible illness whether it's similar in nature to mine physically with the Lyme disease or be it mentally, emotionally, or spiritually. Invisible illness doesn't discriminate, and we all are in this together. I desire to encourage others to not be a spectator in their own life and not accept whatever life throws at them. We have a choice.

It is a sacrifice to live a life of disease and ill health and many times we become the struggle instead of separating our circumstances from our identity. Our identity is in Christ alone. We have His DNA when we are Born Again. Don't believe the lie that illness or disease is God's best for you. Don't say it and claim it for yourself. Don't give power to the diagnosis.

God had a work to do in my inner self as well as my outer self. My soul was broken because I lost my peace. That peace was already within me in seed form because the Bible says in Galatians 5:22 that it's a fruit of the spirit. I needed to maintain it from within and release it. That's how it grows. When we walk in peace, we remain stable in our soul, and we are powerful against anything the Enemy may come against us with. Stress overload and pressure can rob us from peace ruling in our hearts and minds and that leads to brokenness. The word Shalom means "wholeness." Colossians 3:15 tells us to let "peace rule in our hearts." It is our referee. We need to go back to the basics every time our mind becomes divided between faith and fear and tell our soul to be still and trust God (Psalm 46:10).

My heart breaks for anyone finding themselves in a position of invisible illness. Please know that you are not alone! Read that again. You are NOT alone! It may feel like it now but remember that feelings can rise and fall on a whim. We are called Believers for a reason and not "feelers!" Take time to acknowledge those feelings and process through them making sure to use God's filter of truth to replace the lies.

Battling illness is arduous and awful. It can leave you in a hopeless state and one that spouses, family members, and friends wish they could help with, but they can't. Until you've walked a road where even drinking filtered water causes your body to spark symptoms and illness, it's hard to relate to anyone. It's excruciatingly LONELY! I share this because I often feel that some of us living this type of life are treated as if it's a spiritual or physical matter only and guilt and shame result if we aren't careful. It's often a combination of both because we live in a fallen world. I hope my story encourages you to do your part as God leads in order that you may receive your full inheritance that Jesus died to give you!

What if I am not a Christian?

Jesus is ready to receive you just as you are, TODAY, so keep reading.

One day, we all will give account for our life here on earth, the Bible tells us and that "every knee will bow in heaven and on earth and under the earth, and every tongue confess that Jesus Christ is Lord" (Philippians 2:10).

Accepting Jesus as your Personal Savior

It is through Grace by Faith that we are saved. There's only ONE way and His name is JESUS!

> "For God so loved the world that he gave his one and only son that whosoever BELIEVES in him shall not perish but have everlasting life" (John 3:16).

Eternal life is a free gift; no earning it by good works; it was all done on the cross.

> "For it is by GRACE you have been saved, through faith and this not from yourselves, it is the gift of God-not by works, so that no one can boast" (Ephesians 2:8-9).

> "For all have sinned and fall short of the glory of God" (Romans 3:23).

> "For the wages of sin is death, but the gift of God is eternal life in Christ Jesus our Lord" (Romans 6:23).

"Everyone who calls on the name of the Lord will
be saved" (Romans 10:13).

1- Pray–Confess with your mouth that you're a sinner and
need a Savior. Tell Him that you believe in your heart that He
died on the cross to save you from your sins, and He is the only
way to get to Heaven and live forever with Him. Thank Him for
what He's done and that your sins are forgiven now because of
the blood He shed for you on the cross. Receive that forgiveness
and release your faith that now you are a child of God, and the
old nature has gone and the new has come.

Congratulations and welcome to the family!

It's the GREATEST gift you will ever receive, and it will
change your life in amazing ways! You will know that once you
leave this Earth you'll be forever living in Heaven with God and
those gone before you who also are Believers. Your life may still
be messy but now you'll have hope in every area of that mess. In
every problem, there will be a redemptive solution and your life
will now have meaning and purpose way beyond this perishing
earth. Jesus is the Anchor for your soul and Creator of solutions
to every one of your problems before they ever appear.

"Jesus answered, I AM the WAY, the TRUTH,
and the LIFE! No one comes to the Father but
through Him" (John 14:6).

All these promises are now yours once you enter into a relationship with Jesus and the journey begins with God the Father,
God the Son, and God the Holy Spirit. You'll wonder how and
why you ever went a day without Him.

Now that you're going to Heaven to spend eternity with God once you pass from this earth, your new race begins just as you received Jesus-by grace through faith.

Run in such a way as to get the Prize!

Pray and get into the Word of God! When God gives you a promise, continue declaring that over your life not letting the Enemy trick you into believing it was all a lie. When bad circumstances come, fight back with what God has spoken.

Abraham in Romans 4:17-21 received a covenantal promise with God that he would be the Father of all nations. He faced the fact that his body was good as dead at 100 years old of producing the son God promised.

- He didn't weaken in his faith
- He didn't waver through unbelief regarding the promise of God
- He was strengthened in faith and gave glory to God
- He was fully persuaded by God's power to do what He promised He would do

The key is living a life of deepening roots. Hold on to your promise and don't let anyone or anything take it from you. It may take a long time for it to come to pass, but God never lies and will do what He promises He will do. How do we do this? We stay in faith and trust God's Word. Every time our fleshly mind doubts and fears, we combat the Enemy's lies with the promises of truth in scripture and what the Holy Spirit tells us.

I continue holding onto my promise of COMPLETE HEALING! Much of it has come to pass already in my spirit, soul, and body by working together with God and yet there's still more I am believing for. He promises to give us double for our trouble (Hosea 1:15; Job 42:10; Isaiah 61:4; Joel 2:25) so get in the Word, worship by taking time every day to delight in His presence, and enjoy the relationship to the King of the Universe and our very own loving Abba Father! There's nothing else that can satisfy, and my deepest heart's desire is that you too will love the Lord our God with all your heart, mind, soul, and strength!

Keep running YOUR race and finish strong, my friend! When you're ready to quit, find your second wind and take that next step of faith.

References

Dr. Alex. "The Healing Code." Dr Alexander Lloyd. January, 2022. dralexanderlloyd.com

Dr. Leaf. "21 Day Brain Detox." Dr. Caroline Leaf. January, 2022. drleaf.com

EMDR International Association. "About EMDR Therapy." Emdria. October, 2021. emdria.org/about-emdr-therapy

Global Lyme Alliance. February, 2022. globallymealliance.org/about-lyme/prevention/2022

IGeneX Inc. "About Genus Borrelia – Lyme Disease." Igenex. February, 2022. Igenex.com/disease/borrelia/

International Lyme and Associated Diseases Educational Foundation. "Frequently Asked Questions about Lyme Disease." ILADEF. March, 2022. iladef.org/education/lyme-disease-faq/

Johns Hopkins Medicine. "Ticks and Lyme Disease." March, 2022. Hopkinsmedicine.org/health/conditions-and-disease/lyme-disease/ticks-and-lymedisease

ifm.org/functionalmedicine

Leaf, Caroline. "Bring Toxic Thoughts into Captivity." YouTube video. June 4, 2014. youtube.com/watch?v=ZczIP_79jXs

Lyme Awareness of Cape Cod. "Preventative Mcasures." Lyme Ticks. March, 2022. Lymeticks.org/prevention

Purohit, Dhru. "Broken Brain." Dr. Hyman. March, 2022. drhyman.com/brokenbrain/

CPSIA information can be obtained
at www.ICGtesting.com
Printed in the USA
BVHW032232040623
665285BV00006B/122